Riddles,
Tongue Twisters,
and other
Silly Stuff

This edition published in 2019 by Arcturus Publishing Limited
26/27 Bickels Yard, 151–153 Bermondsey Street,
London SE1 3HA

Written by Lisa Regan
Illustrations by Moreno Chiacchiera and Small World Design
Design by Notion Design and Marie Everitt

CH006974NT
Supplier 40, Date 0719, Print run 9005

Printed in the UK

Introduction

On the following pages, you'll find baffling brain-teasers, cunning conundrums, and ridiculous riddles that will give your mental muscles a real workout! The solutions can be straightforward, or they might require some head-scratching. Some will make you laugh, while others are sure to make you groan. Remember, all the answers are in the back, but try not to peek! Now it's time to get riddling!

⭐ I. Natural beauty

Starting at the arrow, follow the compass clues to reveal something pretty in the sky!

6 squares East   ___

1 square North   ___

5 squares West   ___

2 squares North   ___

3 squares East   ___

3 squares North   ___

3 squares West   ___

_ _ _ _ _ _ _

W	R	G	O	J	D	C
A	Y	D	H	K	Q	S
G	B	E	H	R	L	Z
N	H	D	B	J	M	Q
J	R	Q	Z	T	E	M
I	A	L	J	I	A	S
X	Q	L	S	G	R	E

START →

Answers on page 217

2. What food sounds like a frightened person?

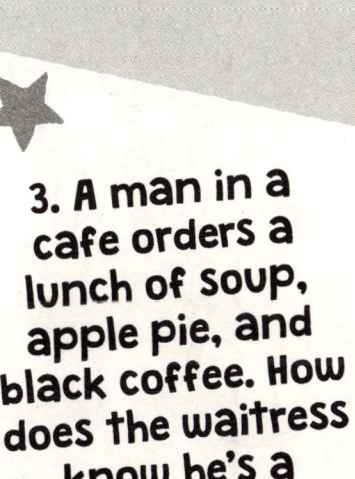

3. A man in a cafe orders a lunch of soup, apple pie, and black coffee. How does the waitress know he's a policeman?

4. You throw away the outside and cook the inside. Then you eat the outside and throw away the inside. What is it?

5. What is black when you buy it, red when you're making dinner, and silvery when you throw it away?

6. Two pirates are standing on opposite sides of a ship. One looks west and the other east, yet they can see each other clearly. How is that?

7. What comes down but never goes up?

8. Elephants have two, but I have only one; flippers are my arms, legs, I have none. Although I'm a mammal, on land I'm never found; I live where it's coldest, the whole year round. What am I?

9. Number count

Fill in the grid so that each row, column, and mini-square contains a number from 1 to 4.

4			
		1	
	2	4	
		2	1

10. Home, sweet home

Break the code to reveal the type of home this little bird is standing on.

— — — — — — — —
8 1 20 13 7 18 21 3

Answers on page 217

11. Recipe:
Take one season.
Add seasoning.
Roll it over and over.
What do you get?

12. I make my mark on book or card, but I will break if you press too hard.

13. What has hands but no fingers, a face but no eyes, and moves all the time without leaving the spot?

14. If your mother carries three bags of groceries into the house, and she makes you carry six bags, who has the heaviest load?

15. Go on red, and stop on green. Your teeth will know just what I mean. What am I?

16. What food starts off hard but gets softer and goes bang as it changes?

17. Yummy cake

Follow the trail and write down every second letter to find a type of cake.

O B A R M O F
E Z I L N K W F
E D S H

‗‗ ‗‗ ‗‗ ‗‗ ‗‗ ‗‗ ‗‗ ‗‗ ‗‗

18. What's left?

Cross out 4 insects, 4 sea creatures, and 4 sports in the selection below. What connects the remaining words?

STARFISH

SHARK   KATY

DRAGONFLY
                    WHALE

SEAL
          WASP   RACHEL

KELLY
          LADYBIRD

BASEBALL

          ANT   SOCCER

SWIMMING   HOCKEY

Answers on page 218

19. I touch the Earth, I touch the sky, but if I touch you, you'll surely die.

20. My feet stay warm, but my head is cold. No one can move me, I'm just too old.

21. I rest near the shore, never touching the sea. I bring worlds together, yet people cross me.

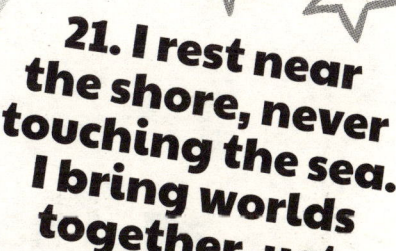

22. From my mouth belch black clouds and red-hot rain. You could sail upon my river, but your ship would be in flame.

23. Two fathers and two sons are at the supermarket. They want a pizza each, and the store has plenty, but they only buy three. Why is that?

24. I have eyes but cannot see. My jacket is brown, but I don't wear clothes. My skin can be red, white, or brown, but I never need sunscreen. What am I?

25. Sports fans

Timmy, Kate, and David love to play sports. Follow the trails to find out which ones they like best!

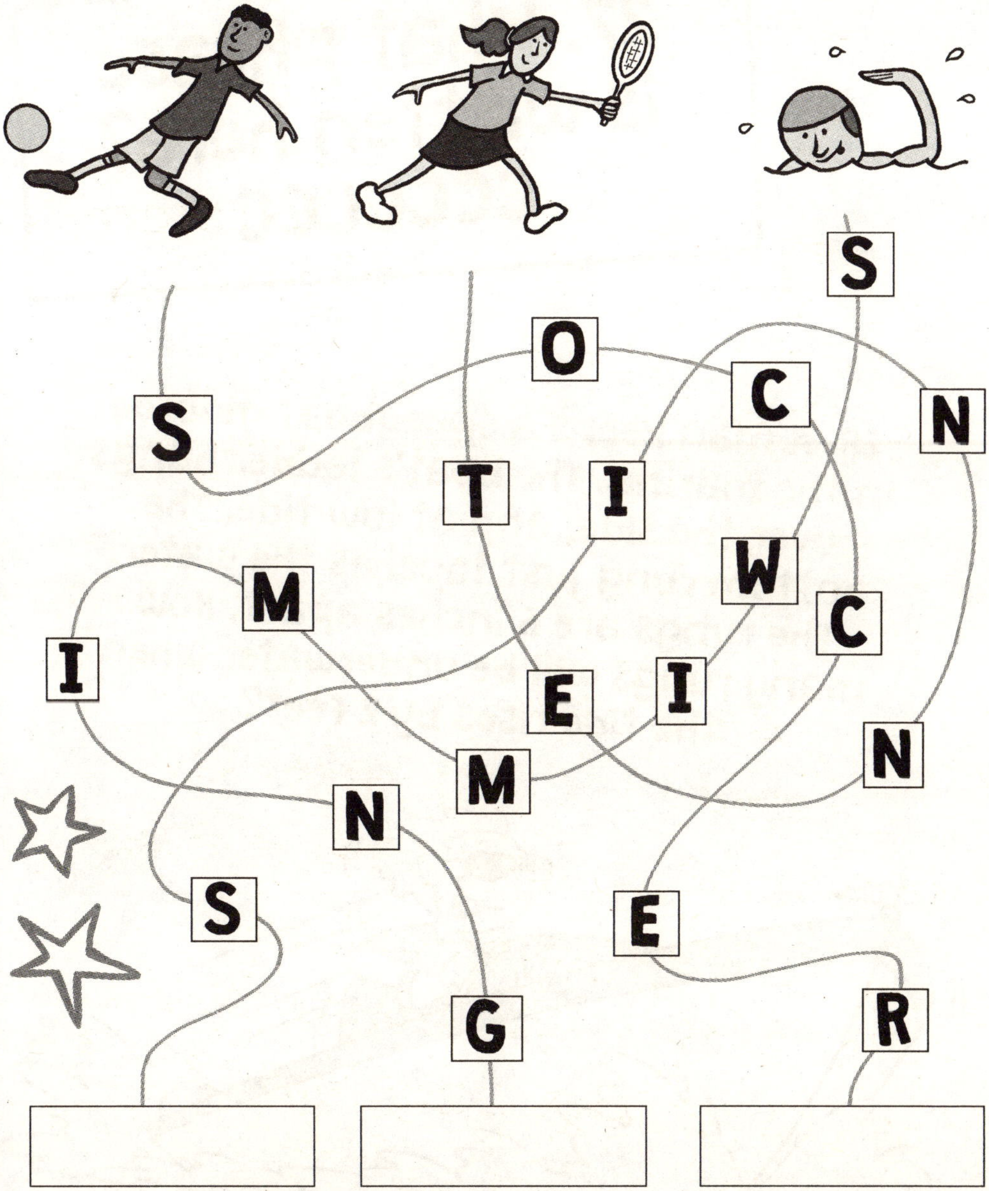
S
O
C
N
S
T
I
W
M
C
I
E
I
N
M
N
S
E
G
R

Answers on page 218

26. What's the difference between an iceberg and a clothes brush?

27. What phrase is written here?
CCCCCCC

28. A man keeps a speedboat moored in the marina. The boat's ladder hangs over the side, and at low tide, the bottom rung just touches the water. The rungs are 6 inches apart. How many rungs will be underwater when the tide rises by 2 feet?

29. Count to 100

There are 5 pairs of numbers that add up to 100 in the grid. Can you circle them?

20	50	50	15	18
5	16	30	60	40
9	80	20	30	15
70	30	50	10	9
8	40	5	90	10

Answers on page 219

30. Little waiter

Follow the start arrow and the compass clues to find a type of bird.

7 squares East ___
1 square North ___
4 squares West ___
2 squares North ___
4 squares East ___
3 squares North ___
6 squares West ___

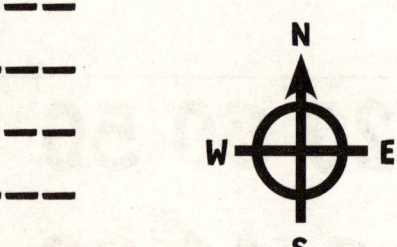

_ _ _ _ _ _ _

N	J	S	Q	Z	L	I
W	S	G	H	L	R	O
B	S	J	L	E	T	A
C	K	G	Q	L	S	U
Y	S	K	E	L	C	I
L	A	N	Q	V	X	E
J	R	S	K	A	U	P

START →

Answers on page 219

31. Imagine you are deep-sea diving. You come face to face with a great white shark. You're terrified! What should you do?

32. What sea creature can swim as fast as it likes, but it never gets away from home?

33. What kind of fish has lots of fans?

34. Charlie's mother has just gone into his bedroom to wake him for school. She asked him a question, and she knows that he lied when he answered. How can she be so sure?

35. A teacher asks: "How many seconds are there in a year?" Amresh says, "Twelve." The teacher thinks for a moment, then says, "Yes, that's correct." How can that be?

36. What does this say?
YYUR
YYUB
ICUR
YY4 me!

37. Destinations

Follow the trails to find out where the bags are headed. Write the answers in the boxes.

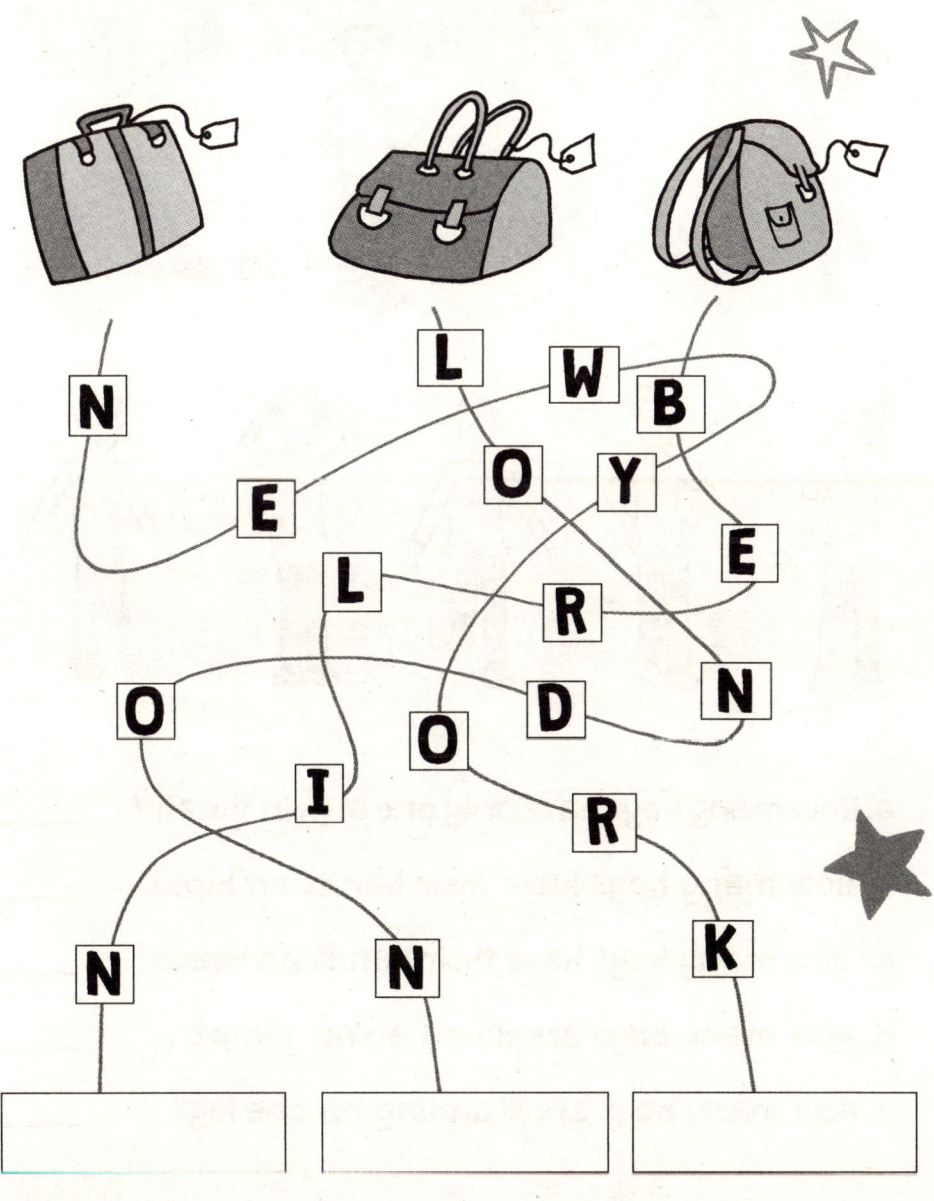

38. In the crowd

Study the boys in gym class and answer the questions below.

a. How many boys have only one arm in the air? ____

b. How many boys have their hands on hips? ____

c. How many boys have their hands on heads? ____

d. How many boys are doing a star jump? ____

e. How many boys are standing on one leg? ____

Answers on page 220

39. What kind of ship would it take to forge an alliance between enemy pirates?

40. What flies through the air using borrowed feathers?

41. Halo of water, Tongue of wood. Skin of stone, For ages, I've stood. What am I?

42. What do giraffes have that no other animal has, that keeps them from going extinct?

43. What type of animal works for the CIA?

24

Answers on page 220

44. Sailing

Study this fleet of yachts heading out to sea and then answer the questions below.

a. How many yachts have numbers on their sails? ____

b. How many yachts have two flags flying? ____

c. How many yachts have three portholes? ____

d. How many yachts have a striped sail? ____

e. How many yachts have letters on their sails? ____

45. Fast cat

Follow the start arrow and the compass clues to find the fastest animal in the world!

5 squares West   ___
2 squares North   ___
2 squares West   ___
2 squares North   ___
4 squares East   ___
2 squares North   ___
4 squares West   ___

_ _ _ _ _ _ _ _

H	W	Q	Q	A	T	O
V	Z	V	L	D	A	J
E	M	X	Y	T	U	X
G	X	K	A	T	P	F
E	W	H	L	R	X	B
J	K	I	K	L	D	R
G	E	C	Z	B	W	U

START ←

46. Dita has bought presents for her two sisters. Both presents do the same thing. One has many moving parts, but the other has none. One works all the time, but the other doesn't work at night. What did she buy?

47. What word begins and ends with an "e" but has only one letter in it?

48. What stays in the corner but travels around the world?

49. Which month has 28 days?

Answers on pages 220-221

50. Is it possible to drop an unboiled egg onto a concrete kitchen floor without cracking it?

51. What two things can you eat but never have for lunch?

52. I am a food with three letters in my name. Lose the last two, and I still sound the same.

Answers on page 221

53. Count to 35

There are 5 pairs of numbers that add up to 35 in the grid. Can you circle them?

2	30	5	15	7
8	4	25	10	3
23	12	11	6	8
4	10	3	27	8
6	21	14	6	9

54. Month mix-up

This calendar has got all muddled!
Break the code to find out which
month it is.

$$\overline{\quad}\ \overline{\quad}\ \overline{\quad}\ \overline{\quad}\ \overline{\quad}\ \overline{\quad}\ \overline{\quad}$$
21   9   26   21   8   11   24

Answers on page 221

55. Mystery Word

Each line of this puzzle is a clue to a letter. Can you discover the hidden word?

My first is in tasty and also in squish.
My second's in ship but isn't in fish.
My third is in pudding and also in rice.
My fourth is in nasty but also in nice.
My fifth is the first of the vowels, it's true.
My sixth is in crunch and in lick and in chew.
My last is in dish but isn't in side, I am really healthy ... you'll eat me with pride!

56. What food has six letters, but if you chop off half of it, you are left only with the item to cook it in?

57. Square riddles

Fill in the grid so that each row, column, and mini-square contains a number from 1 to 4.

2	4		3
	3	4	
			1

Answers on page 222

58. A ship's crew is caught in a tropical storm. They all take shelter, apart from Captain Crick. He braves the elements and the lashing rain. He has no raincoat, no hat, and no umbrella. His clothes are totally soaked, rain drips from the end of his nose, and yet not a hair on his head gets wet. How can this be?

59. What is the strongest creature in the sea?

60. I'm as round as a ball; you can eat my all. I'm delicious with butter and make a nursery for butterflies. What am I?

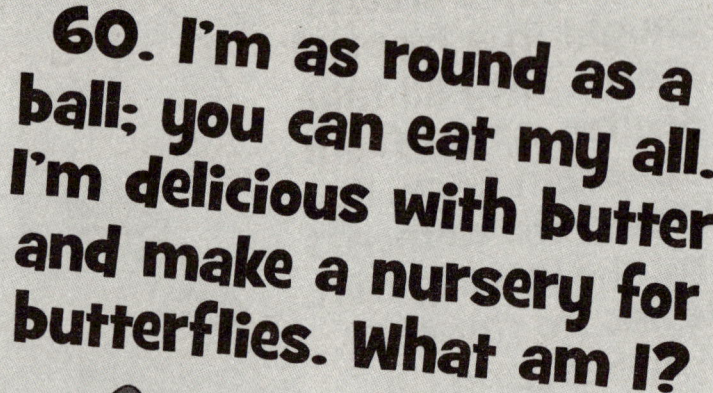

61. What food is written here?
POTOOOOOOOOO

62.
I have the same number of oranges as my friend. How many would I have to give her, so that she has 10 more oranges than I have?

63. Wrap up warm!

Brrr! It's cold outside! Write down every second letter to find something to keep you warm.

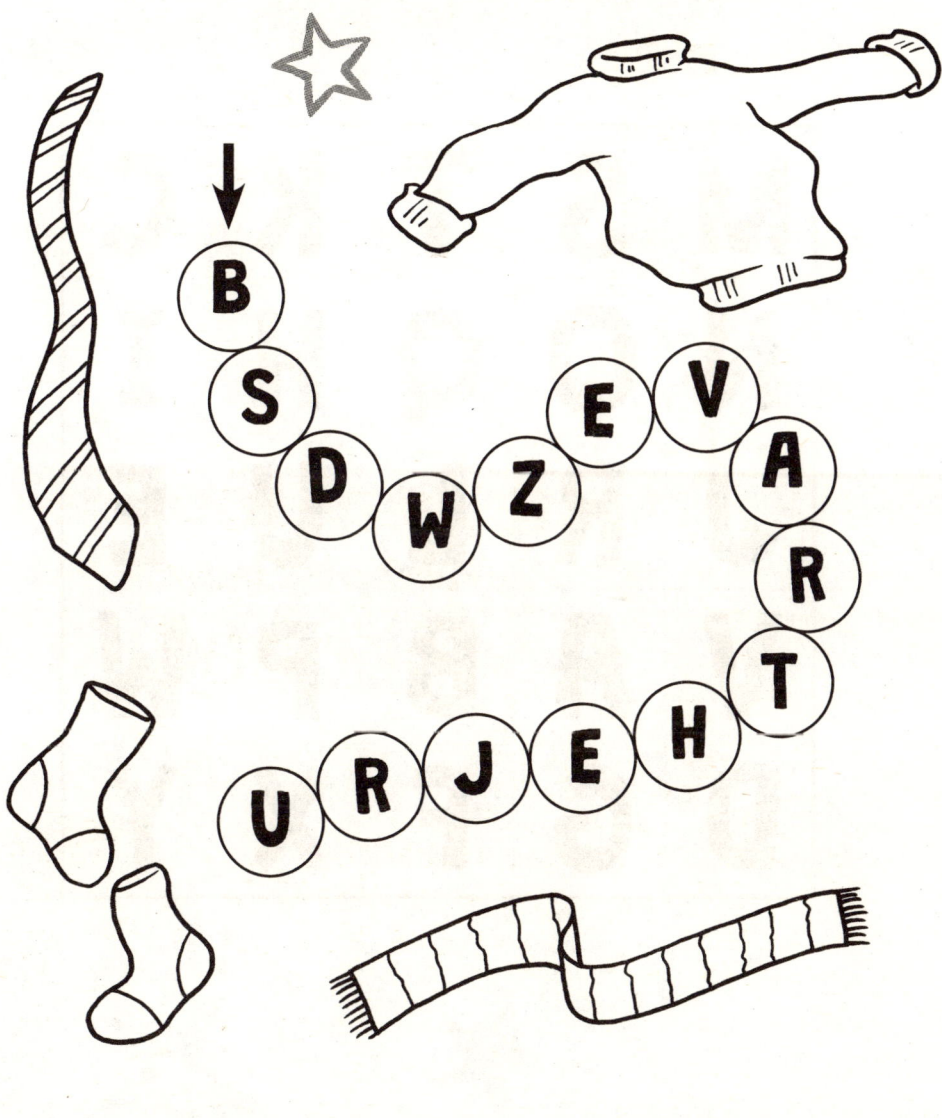

__ __ __ __ __ __ __

64. Perfect pairs

In this grid, there are 5 pairs of letters that sit next to each other in the alphabet. Can you circle them?

M	S	T	K	C
N	O	Q	H	I
J	R	L	U	E
V	A	B	P	W
D	G	F	X	Y

Answers on pages 222-223

65. A monkey is tied to the end of a piece of string 3 feet long. How did it manage to eat some figs from a bowl 9 feet away?

66. What creature walks on four legs in the morning, two legs at noon, and three legs in the evening?

67. When is a rook not a bird?

68. A triangle has three sides, and a square has four. Why might you say that a bubble has two?

69. If you multiply two by itself twenty times, what answer will you get?

70. Mrs. David asked Alex to multiply five numbers together. She read out each, one at a time, but after just one number, he knew the answer. How could that be?

71. Count to 20

There are 5 pairs of numbers that add up to 20 in the grid. Can you circle them?

3	19	1	15	2
16	4	8	10	4
11	2	10	10	2
4	15	5	8	5
10	3	4	14	6

Answers on page 223

72. Maisie was learning about adjectives. She asked her English teacher for help. "Miss Stuart, which is correct: My brother chose the bigger half of the cake or my brother chose the biggest half of the cake?" What did Miss Stuart say?

73. The average English word is five letters long, although it's easy to think of words with more than 10 letters. What is the longest word in the English language?

74. Treasure hunt

Cross out 4 snakes, 4 musical instruments, and 4 types of homes in the selection below. What connects the remaining words?

BUNGALOW

DRUM

COBRA

BOA

RUBY

HOUSE

FLAT

DIAMOND

ANACONDA

VIPER

PIANO

VIOLIN

CABIN

PEARL

FLUTE

75. Count to 30

There are 5 pairs of numbers that add up to 30 in the grid. Can you circle them?

15	15	8	8	10
5	9	10	20	7
7	18	12	5	9
19	4	8	29	1
14	16	8	8	14

Answers on page 224

76. What Is Missing?

How quickly can you find out what is so unusual about this paragraph? It looks so ordinary that you would think that nothing is wrong with it at all, and in fact, nothing is. But it is unusual. Why? If you study it and think about it, you may find out, but I am not going to assist you in any way. You must do it without coaching. No doubt, if you work at it for long, it will dawn on you. Who knows? Go to work, and test your skill!

77. The singular forms of the verb "to be" are: "I am," "you are," and "he, she, or it is." However, can you think of an example where you would be correct in saying, "I is"?

78. In the jungle

Follow the start arrow and the compass clues to find a jungle creature.

5 squares West   _ _ _

2 squares South   _ _ _

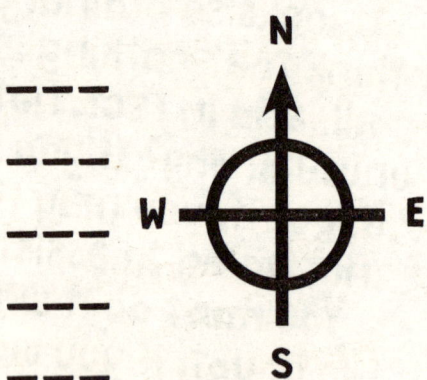

2 squares South   _ _ _

2 squares West   _ _ _

2 squares South   _ _ _

6 squares East   _ _ _

_ _ _ _ _ _ _

START

D	Y	P	K	P	L	C
Z	V	J	K	U	W	M
Q	R	A	G	J	D	C
D	Z	B	M	O	E	L
R	S	R	K	P	W	J
A	Z	P	N	S	B	L
O	R	A	H	K	D	T

79. I hiss like a frying pan and am made with an egg. I can move around, though I have no legs. My skin peels off, but I stay the same. I'm long and strong ... do you know my name?

80. The more you take, the more you leave behind. What are they?

81. Why don't lions eat stand-up comedians?

Answers on page 224

82. This is a very old, traditional riddle:

As I was going to St. Ives, I met a man with seven wives. Each wife had seven sacks, and every sack had seven cats. Every cat had seven kittens. Kittens, cats, wives, sacks: How many were going to St. Ives?

83. If the alphabet goes from A to Z, what goes from Z to A?

Answers on pages 224-225

84. Sum it up

Fill in the grid so that each row, column, and mini-square contains a number from 1 to 4.

	2		
		2	
3		4	
2			1

85. What's my name?

Who are these happy people? Follow the trails to spell out their names, then write them in the boxes.

N   S   W

A   I

H   L   T

O   L

P   L   I

A   H   E   A

N   I   M

Answers on page 225

86. Forward, I am heavy, but backward, I am not. What am I?

87. How would you describe a man who does not have all his fingers on his left hand?

**88. Every dawn begins with me.
At dusk, I'm the first thing you see.
Daybreak couldn't start without what midday's middle is all about.
All through the night, I won't be found, yet in the dark, I'm still around. What am I?**

89. What begins with T, ends with T, and has T in the middle?

90. What cup can't you drink from?

91. Cows drink it, and most people have some in their coffee. What am I thinking of?

92. What has a neck and a bottom but no head?

93. Mystery set

Cross out 4 vehicles, 4 sweet treats, and 4 birds in the selection below. What connects the remaining words?

GOLF

TART

BICYCLE

ROBIN

TRAIN

SCONE

ROOK

SEAGULL

TENNIS DONUT

 CAR OSTRICH BUS

 SQUASH SPONGE

94. Secret numbers

Find the number sequences hidden in the grid. Look up, down, across, and diagonally.

7398	5426	0095	2713	4401
9020	6394	1202	9980	0203

```
1 5 4 4 0 1 3 0 7 6
9 2 5 8 3 8 2 0 4 1
7 3 9 9 4 0 2 5 5 3
2 1 6 3 9 2 7 4 3 0
9 7 5 7 8 0 1 2 0 2
9 2 3 2 6 3 8 6 5 0
0 1 8 9 9 8 0 4 7 0
2 7 4 1 0 6 7 9 2 8
0 0 9 5 2 9 8 5 3 9
1 6 3 4 9 6 3 9 4 5
```

95. This three-letter word means "chew and swallow." Add another letter, and you can use me to cook. Add one more letter, and you can make cereal from me.

96. What has to be broken before it is useful?

97. I wear a crown, but I'm not a king. I have scales, but I'm not a snake. On the outside, I'm tough, but on the inside, I'm sweet. What am I?

Answers on page 226

98. Dizzy digits

Fill in the grid so that each row, column, and mini-square contains a number from 1 to 4.

			1
4			2
2			4
		2	3

Answers on page 226

99. What will you find in the middle of a pie that isn't used in a cake, turnover, or tart?

100. A braggart likes to boast, and a boat sails off from the coast. But what do you put in a toaster?

101. What kind of nut has a hole?

102. Crunchy fruit

Break the code to find out what type of apple this is before the worm eats it all!

$$\overline{13} \quad \overline{24} \quad \overline{7} \quad \overline{20} \quad \overline{20} \quad \overline{5} \qquad \overline{25} \quad \overline{19} \quad \overline{15} \quad \overline{26} \quad \overline{14}$$

Answers on page 227

103. How many bricks does it take to complete a brick barn that is 30 feet by 30 feet by 40 feet and made completely of bricks?

104. I have six legs, four eyes, and five ears. What am I?

105. What always runs but never walks, often murmurs but never talks, has a bed but never sleeps, has a mouth but never eats?

106. Farmer Jones gets home after a long day harvesting. It is dark, and he is cold and hungry. He has a candle, a stove, and a fireplace, but he only has a single match. Which should he light first?

107. I fly through the air with the greatest of ease. And I am also something you do to your peas.

108. The farmer was worried that her prize currant bush would never grow back after a cold winter. What did she say when she saw it was healthy and green?

109. Count to 100

There are 5 pairs of numbers that add up to 100 in the grid. Can you circle them?

20	50	50	15	18
5	16	30	60	40
9	80	20	30	15
70	30	50	10	9
8	40	5	90	10

110. A man goes scuba diving and comes face to face with a tiger. Last year while diving, he met a bull. How can this be?

111. Dave doesn't dare go deep-sea diving in Dominica every year. Can you spell all that without the letter "d"?

112. What is the number one use of shark skin in the world?

Answers on pages 227

113. Woof, woof

Follow the trail and write down every second letter to find a breed of dog.

—— —— —— —— —— —— —— —— —— —— ——

114. Letter pairs

In this grid, there are 5 pairs of letters that sit next to each other in the alphabet. Can you circle them?

D	E	B	F	S
H	M	X	O	P
N	Q	R	V	A
T	U	Z	J	K
G	L	W	C	I

Answers on page 228

115. What letter tastes like chocolate?

116. Katie's mother went shopping for Katie's birthday party. She bought six pizzas, three cucumbers, twelve carrots, six cartons of strawberries, and forty cupcakes. Katie's brother and his friends raided the refrigerator and ate all but two cucumbers, eight carrots, a carton of strawberries, and seven cupcakes. How many carrots were left?

117. What am I?
Tree ... growth ... red.
Me ... mouth ... fed!

118. I spy

Find the number sequences hidden in the grid. Look up, down, across, and diagonally.

3244   4264   9326   2475   8690

6925   2522   6058   1897   3463

```
6 4 7 4 1 4 4 2 6 4
8 6 4 5 9 8 8 6 5 2
5 2 6 9 3 2 6 9 4 4
3 8 9 2 7 5 2 8 1 7
4 9 2 3 4 9 5 6 8 5
9 3 5 6 6 3 9 9 0 0
2 5 2 2 0 5 3 0 5 1
0 2 3 1 5 0 7 4 3 8
5 0 8 4 8 1 1 8 6 6
1 0 1 8 9 7 5 9 9 3
```

119. What flies when it is born, lies around during its lifetime, and runs when it is dead?

120. Red, purple, orange, yellow, blue, and green. No one can touch me, not even a queen. What am I?

121. Daisy wakes up one morning. Without getting up or opening her eyes, she knows that it has been snowing. How is this possible?

Answers on page 228

122. What's written here?
BOLT
TH

123. Flowers grow up in the warmth of summer. This grows down in the cold of winter. What is it?

124. You can feel it, but you can't touch it. You can hear it, but you can't see it. What is it?

125. Ahoy!

Study this pirate crew and answer the questions below.

a. How many pirates have a parrot? _____

b. How many pirates have a cutlass? _____

c. How many pirates have a pistol? _____

d. How many pirates have a hook? _____

e. How many pirates have a wooden leg? _____

Answers on pages 228-229

126. Solar system

Which planets are these? Follow
the star trails to find out!

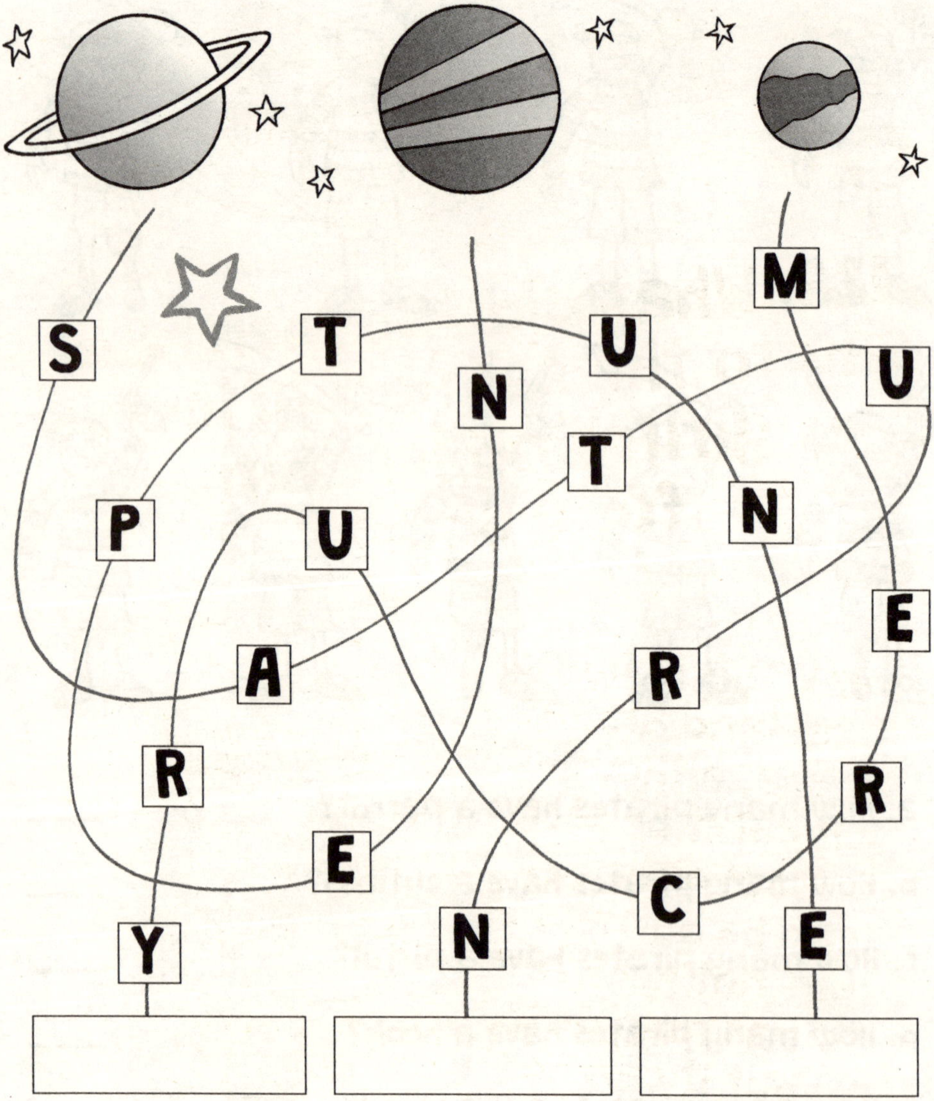

S T N U M

P U N T U

A T N

R R E

Y N C E R

[   ] [   ] [   ]

68

Answers on page 229

127. What am I?
If you can hear where I come from, I am no longer there ...

128. What did the mermaid say to the salmon after his girlfriend left him for a shark?

129. This is found on land and at sea, although it can't be seen from either. It can be harnessed but not held, and it has no mouth, but it can be heard.
What is it?

130. Letter pairs

In this grid, there are 5 pairs of letters that sit next to each other in the alphabet. Can you circle them?

X	P	M	N	T
U	V	R	D	Y
H	E	F	O	S
I	A	Q	K	L
B	C	W	Z	J

Answers on page 229

131. Lizard king

Follow the trail and write down every second letter to find the king of dinosaurs.

__ __ __ __ __ __ __ __ __ __ __ __ __

132. Mystery Word

Each line of this puzzle is a clue to a letter. Can you discover the hidden word?

My first is in cottonwood, in cedar, and in beech.
My second's in banana and also in peach.
My third is in launch and rowing and motion.
My fourth is in swordfish as well as in ocean.
My fifth is in source and also in end.
My whole is a boat you can use with a friend.

133. What has five eyes and runs through the USA?

134. Number magic

Help this sniffer dog find the number sequences hidden in the grid. Look up, down, across, and diagonally.

8122	4873	2809	4059	1715
5532	5463	5528	1369	4238

```
8 1 2 2 0 6 9 1 8 6
4 5 4 6 5 4 3 2 9 9
6 5 8 4 4 8 5 9 6 4
9 4 7 3 6 5 7 4 4 2
5 6 3 8 3 2 4 1 8 3
2 9 9 5 5 3 2 3 5 8
1 8 5 1 8 5 1 6 0 3
0 3 0 4 2 1 0 9 2 0
4 0 5 9 1 7 1 5 1 4
1 5 1 8 7 1 8 0 4 9
```

135. Slippery game

Follow the trail and write down every second letter to find a board game.

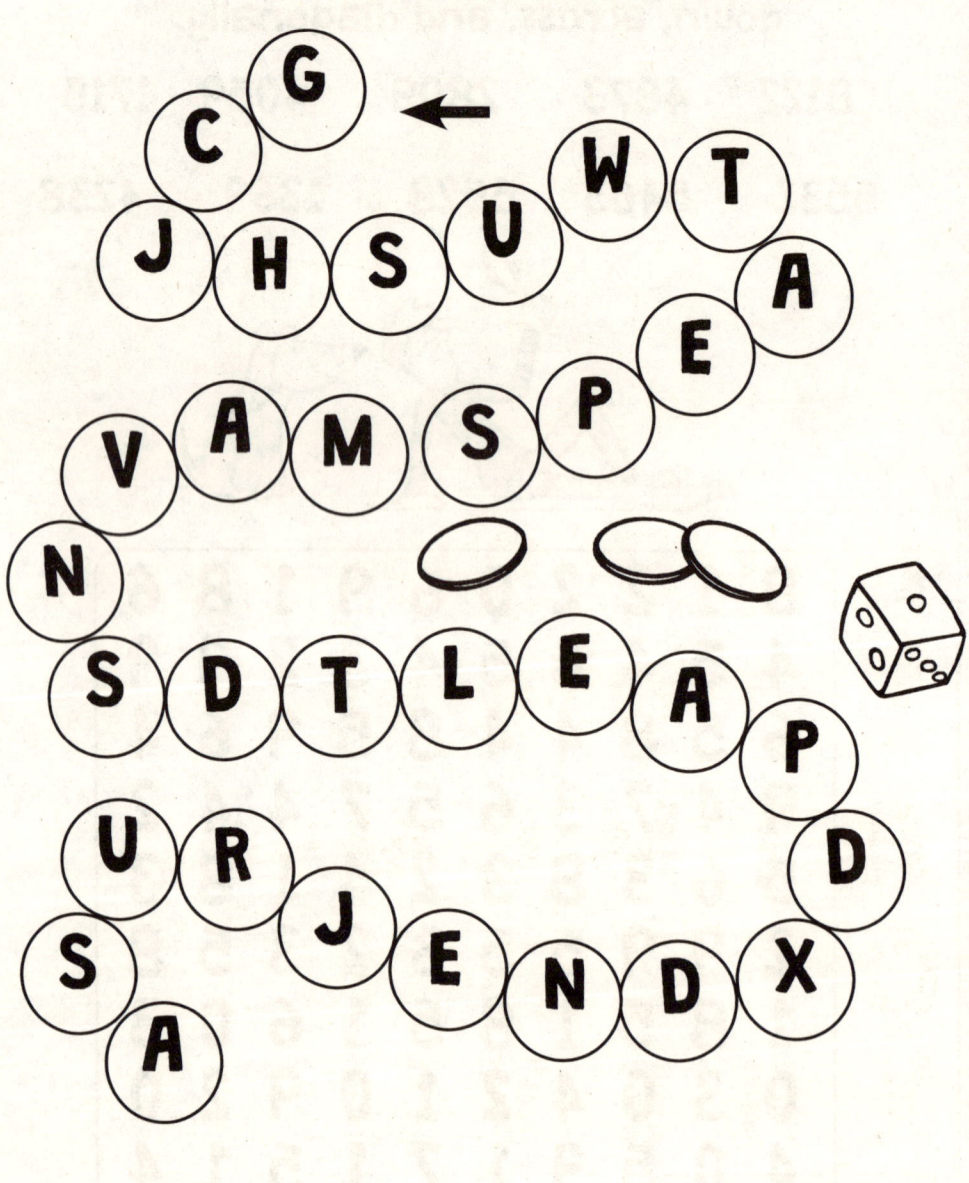

__ __ __ __ __ __ __ __ __

__ __ __ __ __ __ __

136. Hidden letters

In this grid, there are 5 pairs of letters that sit next to each other in the alphabet. Can you circle them?

L N R S P
I J D F G
A T M C U
O Y Z B K
X H E V W

Answers on page 230

137. Count to 45

There are 5 pairs of numbers that add up to 45 in the grid. Can you circle them?

40	5	15	10	4
5	25	20	12	6
8	15	7	30	15
35	10	10	8	14
11	4	28	17	5

Answers on pages 230–231

138. Busy bodies

Cross out 4 wild animals, 4 fruits, and
4 spices in the selection below.
What connects the remaining words?

MONKEY

VANILLA

CINNAMON  **PEAR**

 **GIRAFFE**

NUTMEG

 **APPLE**   **ANT**

BEE   **ORANGE**

 **GINGER**   **TIGER**   **WASP**

 **BANANA**  **SNAKE**

139. If a fisherman brings home 20 buckets of fish, and his father brings home 40 buckets, who has the most fish?

140. What never gets any wetter, no matter how hard it rains?

141. What happens when you throw a white shell into the Red Sea?

Answers on page 231

142. Break the code

Find the number sequences hidden in the grid. Look up, down, across, and diagonally.

1098	5212	9209	9280	3435
4068	9575	9386	4714	5347

```
1 8 2 9 6 0 4 7 1 4
3 0 1 0 9 8 9 2 5 4
4 2 5 7 6 0 5 2 1 2
0 5 6 1 2 3 9 8 7 9
9 6 4 9 8 1 7 3 1 3
2 5 7 2 5 7 7 4 6 9
8 3 4 5 3 4 7 3 5 3
0 1 0 1 9 5 7 5 4 8
7 3 6 2 6 4 1 6 3 6
2 7 8 0 1 1 9 6 7 5
```

143. Sir what?

He's got his helmet on so you'll have to break the code to identify this legendary knight.

$$\overline{}\ \overline{}\ \overline{}\ \overline{}\ \overline{}\ \overline{}\ \overline{}\ \overline{}$$
18 7 20 9 11 18 21 26

Answers on page 231

144. Mount Everest was measured in 1856, but wasn't climbed until 1953. What was the world's highest mountain before then?

145. What is the capital of Antarctica?

146. What has four eyes and a mouth, and runs but has no legs?

147. Where is the best place in the USA to learn your multiplication tables?

148. Smelly veg

Follow the start arrow and the compass clues to catch up with this stinky chap.

5 squares West ___
2 squares North ___
4 squares East ___
3 squares North ___
6 squares West ___
1 square North ___

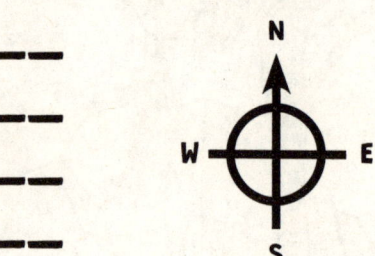

_ _ _ _ _ _

C	W	H	M	L	D	S
I	U	K	P	W	V	L
G	J	T	L	Q	Z	I
Q	Z	H	Y	S	K	W
X	V	A	J	Q	I	R
S	E	Q	X	A	Z	M
W	K	G	T	Z	K	W

START ←

149. Two's company, and three's a crowd, so what do four and five make?

150. Mystery Word

Each line of this puzzle is a clue to a different letter. Can you discover the hidden word?

My first is in add but not
in subtract.
My second is in picked but isn't
in packed.
My third is in over and vacuum and five.
My fourth is in child and bright and alive.
My fifth is in good but is
also in bad.
My last is in made but isn't
in mad.
My whole is about learning to share things out.
Just ask your teacher what I'm all about.

Answers on page 231

151. Which athlete reaches the top of his or her game and is happy that it's all downhill from there?

152. What sport uses a hard, white ball and begins with a "T"?.

153. Mr. Jennings the PE teacher is one of the 36% of teachers in his school who are left-handed. However, he plays racket sports right-handed. Which hand does he use to stir his coffee?

154. Mystery figures

Fill in the grid so that each row, column, and mini-square contains a number from 1 to 4.

	2	1	
		3	2
	1		
2			1

155. What kind of tree can you carry in your hand?

156. Mystery money

Follow the start arrow and the compass clues to find the name of a currency.

3 squares East   ___
1 square North   ___
4 squares East   ___
3 squares North   ___
6 squares West   ___
2 squares North   ___

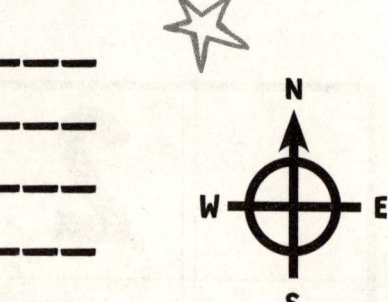

_ _ _ _ _ _ _ _

R	H	K	O	E	C	V
W	Q	Z	J	L	R	D
A	G	U	W	A	M	L
O	L	W	X	Z	Q	H
E	I	X	U	J	P	W
Q	Z	O	U	E	L	L
S	K	D	X	M	S	P

START →

Answers on page 232

157. Count to 40
There are 5 pairs of numbers that add up to 40 in the grid. Can you circle them?

20	20	8	10	6
6	11	9	30	10
5	25	15	10	4
1	22	18	6	11
12	4	32	8	8

158. What's wrong with a story that's set on a Saturday and Sunday?

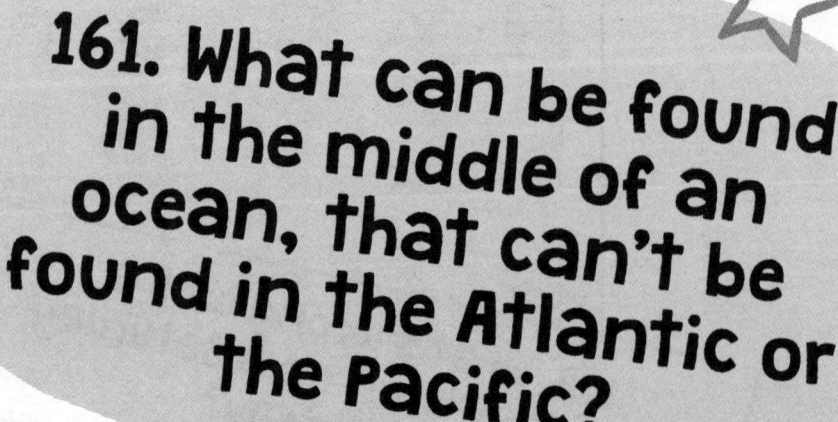

159. Two dolphins are playing in the ocean. Dolphin A is behind dolphin B, but dolphin B is behind dolphin A. How can that be?

160. I am strong enough to walk on and heavy enough to crush roofs. But just a little sunlight will make me vanish! What am I?

161. What can be found in the middle of an ocean, that can't be found in the Atlantic or the Pacific?

162. Find the letters

In this grid, there are 5 pairs of letters that sit next to each other in the alphabet. Can you circle them?

P	Q	T	U	O
V	Z	B	G	H
A	K	I	S	N
F	C	D	J	E
W	X	R	L	M

163. Number teasers

Find the number sequences hidden in the grid. Look up, down, across, and diagonally.

2906	3874	5088	3208	4239
5102	7216	3272	7712	2495

```
2 5 6 1 8 2 4 7 3 9
6 6 4 4 2 3 9 2 1 4
3 2 7 2 3 7 5 9 7 1
5 2 9 8 8 0 9 0 6 5
0 5 4 7 7 1 7 6 2 2
8 1 7 9 4 3 4 1 8 9
8 9 5 7 5 1 7 3 6 0
3 5 1 0 2 7 7 2 1 6
7 8 2 9 1 4 1 0 0 2
1 0 3 1 9 0 9 8 9 6
```

164. Wriggly reptiles

These snakes have come out to bask in the sun. Look at them closely and answer the questions below.

a. How many snakes have spots? ____

b. How many snakes have stripes? ____

c. How many snakes have tongues sticking out? ____

d. How many snakes have triangles? ____

e. How many snakes have fangs? ____

Answers on page 233

165. I sing when I'm struck or whenever they shake me. By careful casting, the craftsmen make me.

166. What do you break just by saying its name?

167. What do you call a man who stands outside the front door all day?

168. Black and white?

Cross out 4 farm animals, 4 countries, and 4 fish in the selection below. What connects the remaining words?

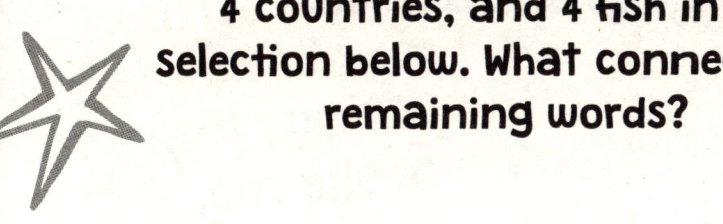

COW

ENGLAND BLUE

HADDOCK FRANCE

SHEEP

GREEN

SPAIN

COD

RED

SKATE NORWAY

SALMON

BULL

DUCK

Answers on page 233

169. Down in the woods

Study this woodland carefully and answer the questions below.

a. How many trees have birds in them?   ____

b. How many trees are losing their leaves?   ____

c. How many trees have a hole in the trunk?   ____

d. How many trees have apples?   ____

e. How many trees have a squirrel in them?   ____

Answers on page 234

170. Why are leopards no good at hiding?

171. Mystery Word

Each line of this puzzle is a clue to a letter.
Can you discover the hidden word?

My first is in wild, and bellow, and water.
My second's in woman and also in daughter.
My third is the very beginning of rough.
My fourth is in bristles, in tusks,
and in tough.
My fifth is in hairy and cough
but not snout.
You're well on your way to working this out!
My sixth appears twice in the roots
that I munch.
My last is in pig, who's one of my bunch.
What am I?

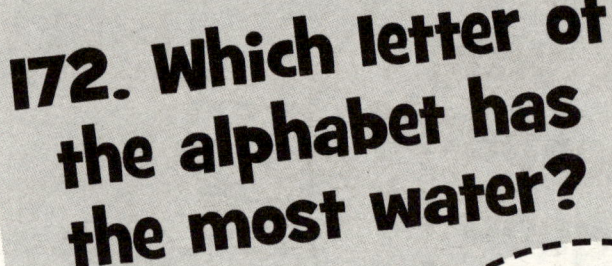

172. Which letter of the alphabet has the most water?

173. Four men were on a fishing trip. A storm blew up and capsized their boat, throwing all of them into the ocean. When they were rescued, every single man was still dry. Why is that?

174. What kind of house weighs the least?

175. Get dressed

Follow the trails to spell out three pieces of clothing. Write the answers in the boxes.

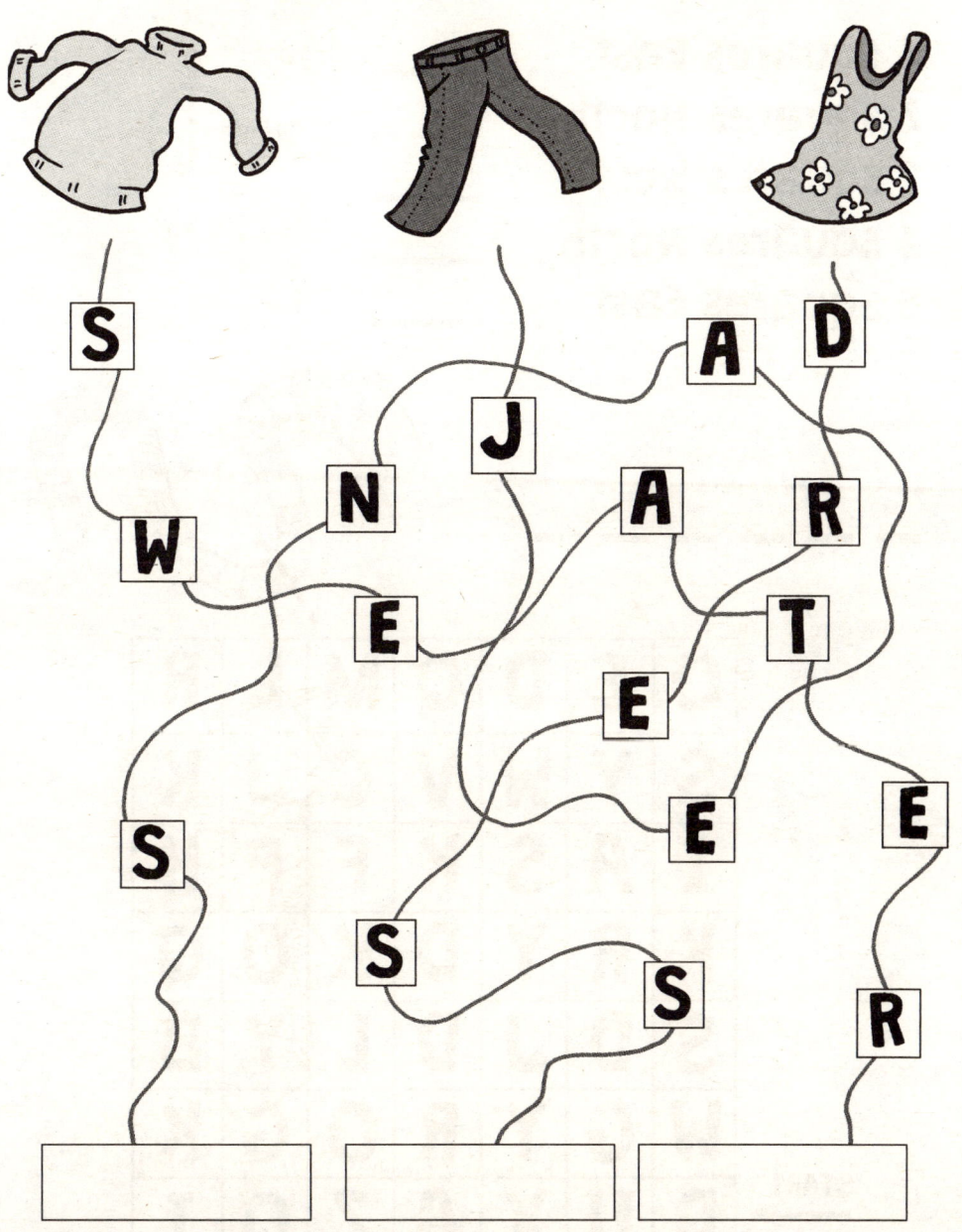

176. Slithery snake

This lurking snake has a nasty bite! Follow the start arrow and the compass clues to reveal what it is.

4 squares East   ___
2 squares North   ___
2 squares West   ___
4 squares North   ___
5 squares East   ___

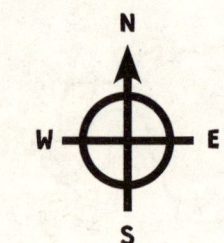

_ _ _ _ _ _

O	E	D	Q	M	L	R
S	Y	W	V	C	J	K
I	A	S	K	F	P	H
K	R	Y	D	K	O	Q
S	D	J	D	L	Y	B
W	G	Y	R	O	G	K
D	U	X	A	Z	Q	I

START →

177. Can you find a way to make 1,000 with eight "8"s and four plus signs?

178. Which number, when written as a word, has its letters in alphabetical order? (For example, it isn't two, since the "o" comes before "t" and "w" in the alphabet.)

179. I'm a kind of learning you just don't get at school. Teachers love me, but pupils think I'm cruel. Your parents might help if they are cool! What am I?

Answers on page 234

180. What single letter can you swap to make a cold bear become hot?

181. What gets naked to keep you warm?

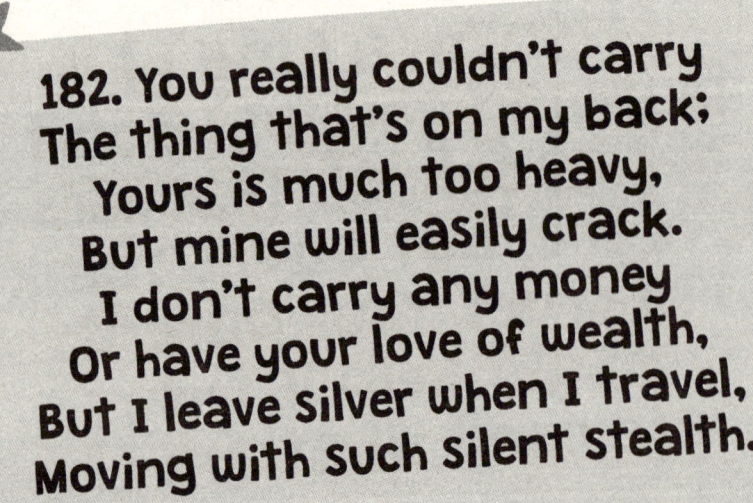

182. You really couldn't carry
The thing that's on my back;
Yours is much too heavy,
But mine will easily crack.
I don't carry any money
Or have your love of wealth,
But I leave silver when I travel,
Moving with such silent stealth.

183. Count to 50

There are 5 pairs of numbers that add up to 50 in the grid. Can you circle them?

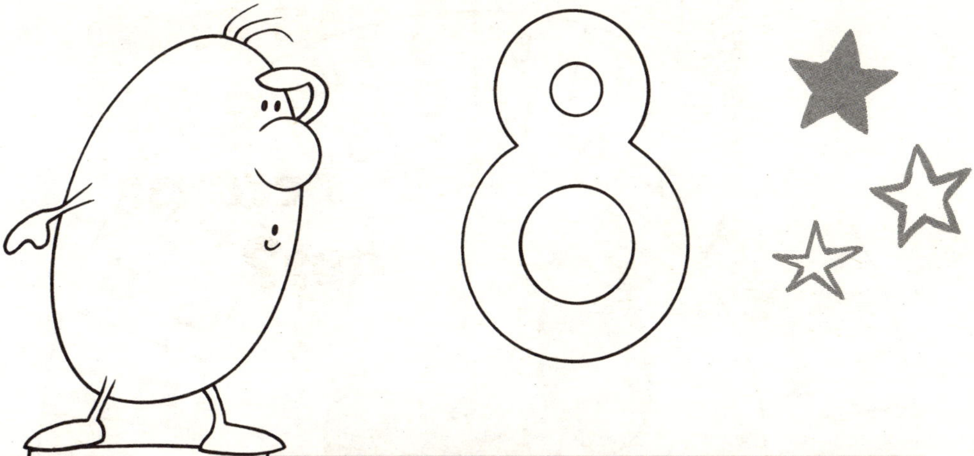

10	25	25	8	11
10	7	40	10	10
30	20	9	14	2
3	12	35	15	4
12	3	42	8	8

Answers on pages 234-235

184. Horsey business
Break the code to find a handsome horse.

‾‾ ‾‾ ‾‾ ‾‾ ‾‾   ‾‾ ‾‾ ‾‾ ‾‾ ‾‾ ‾‾
8 18 7 9 17   8 11 7 1 26 5

Answers on page 235

185. Hot wheels

Follow the trail and write down every second letter to find a type of car.

S L Y I K M P

B S V U R O

I

Z N A E H

_ _ _ _ _ _ _ _ _ _

186. How many ancient philosophers were born in Greece?

187. Why couldn't a centurion living in Roman Britain be legally buried in France?

188. A history teacher shows the class two coins. One is a silver coin with the date 368 BCE, and the other is a bronze coin dated CE 798. Which one is worth the most?

Answers on page 235

189. Square the numbers

Fill in the grid so that each row, column, and mini-square contains a number from 1 to 4.

4		2	1
			3
	2	3	

190. Triple letters

In this grid, there are 4 sets of 3 letters that sit next to each other in the alphabet. Can you circle them?

G	H	I	L	N
D	E	P	Q	R
O	T	Y	K	U
M	A	B	C	S
V	W	X	F	J

Answers on page 236

191. Mystery Word

Each line of this puzzle is a clue to a letter. Can you discover the hidden word?

My first is in ran but isn't in far.
My second's in sea but isn't in star.
My third is in scallop and porpoise and pearl.
My fourth's in typhoon, in twist, and in twirl.
My fifth's in kahuna and also outside.
My first now comes back again, like the tide.
My last is in water and ocean and home.
My whole is a god from mythical Rome.

192. How is the letter "t" like an island?

193. Some kids are playing hide-and-seek. One of them is the seeker. What is the smallest number of children hiding if: a girl is hiding to the left of a boy; a boy is hiding to the left of a boy; two boys are hiding to the right of a girl.

194. How many times does the letter "o" appear in the following sentence?
"Boys often play football at school, and girls often choose to play hockey."

195. What am I thinking of? I can take away the whole and still have some left.

196. Tutti frutti

Follow the trail and write down every second letter to find a juicy fruit.

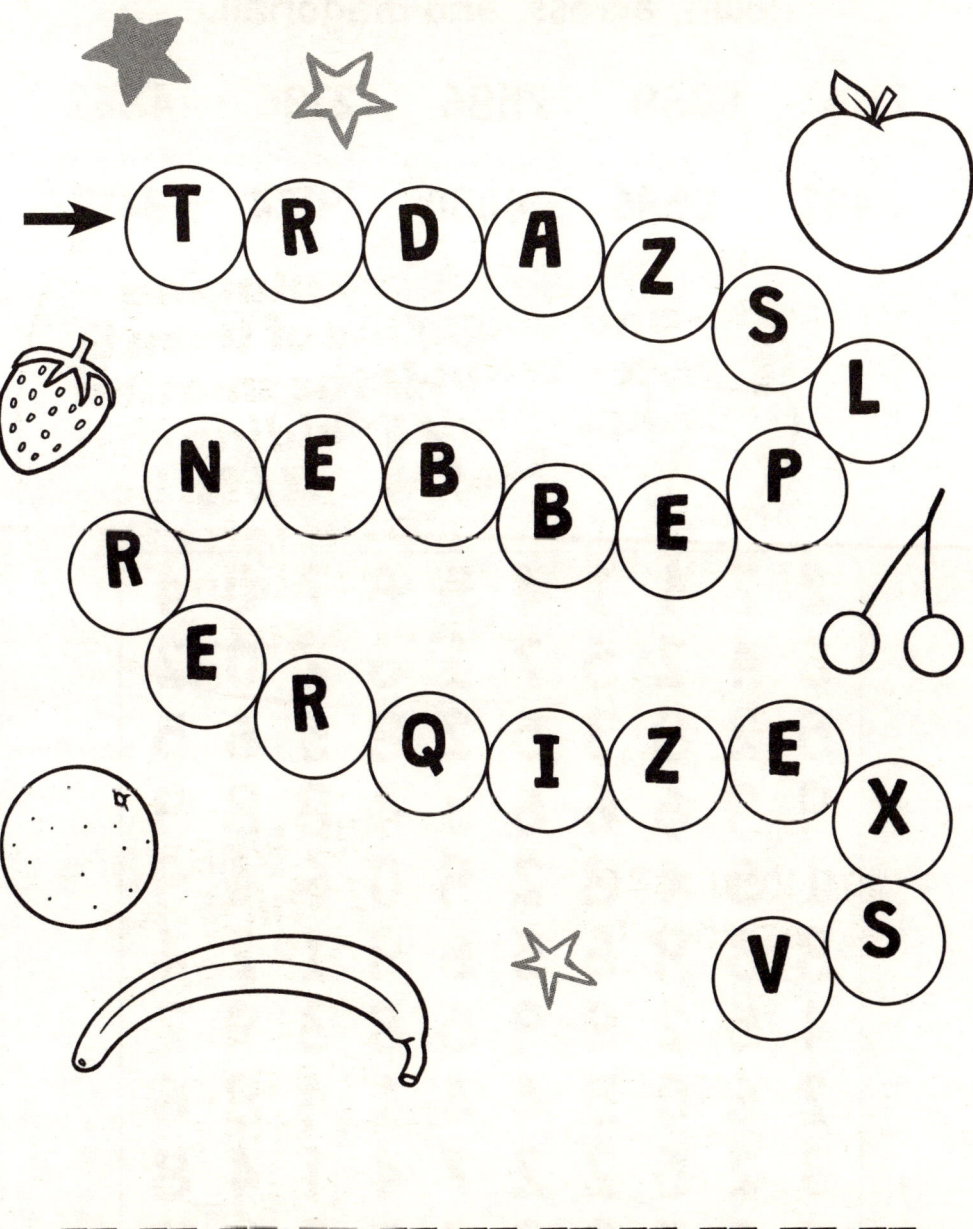

--- --- --- --- --- --- --- --- --- ---

197. Number quiz

Help Ben and Rover find the number sequences hidden in the grid. Look up, down, across, and diagonally.

7114   0068   7586   2396   4862

6492   5596   4030   9124   3412

```
2 7 1 1 4 5 6 7 0 4
6 4 2 5 7 1 6 7 0 2
5 2 8 3 5 2 8 5 6 5
9 9 6 6 6 3 4 8 8 9
1 5 4 8 2 9 0 6 4 9
8 3 9 6 5 6 9 1 2 4
4 5 2 9 9 5 8 3 9 7
2 6 0 5 4 4 1 4 8 6
3 2 5 2 2 7 4 1 4 8
4 0 3 0 8 8 5 2 3 5
```

Answers on page 236

198. Mystery Word

Each line of this puzzle is a clue to a letter.
Can you discover the hidden word?

My first is in bread but never in dear.
My second's in yell and also in cheer.
My third is in duffle and also in hood.
My fourth is in word but isn't in wood.
My fifth and my sixth are letters the same.
A baboon and a rooster have two
in their name.
My last is in temper, moody, and slam.
My whole is at home. Do you know
where I am?

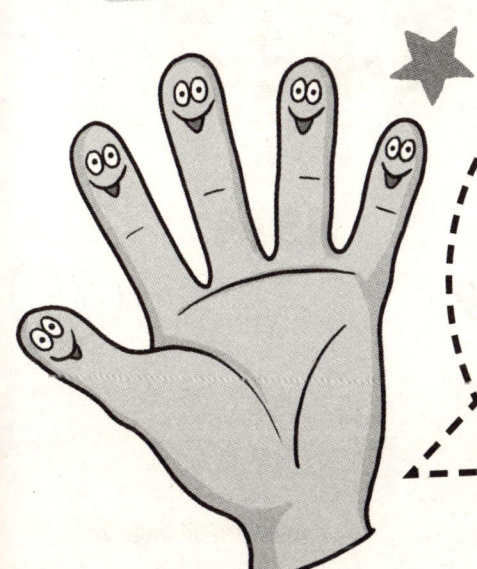

199. What advice do you get from your hands?

200. Healthy mix

Cross out 4 types of dogs, 4 continents, and 4 reptiles in the selection below. What connects the remaining words?

RATTLESNAKE

BOXER

PYTHON

TERRIER

AMERICA

LEEKS

AFRICA

LIZARD

SPANIEL

ONIONS

TORTOISE

EUROPE

CARROTS

GREYHOUND

ASIA

Answers on page 237

201. A zoologist is walking through a jungle and finds something in her pocket. It has a tail and a head but no legs. How does she know it's not dangerous?

202. An explorer is paddling up a river, when he comes to a place where it splits two ways. One way leads to a city of gold, and the other way leads to a waterfall! He has two guides with him. One guide can only tell the truth, and the other always lies. But he doesn't know which is which. What question should the explorer ask to make sure he takes the right route?

203. There are 25 mice in a school classroom during a class. The mice are moving around, but nobody is looking at them. Why is that?

204. What kind of pet always lives on the floor?

205. What did the dentist say to the mouse when it broke a tooth?

206. Thirsty work!

Follow the trails to spell out three delicious drinks. Write the answers in the boxes.

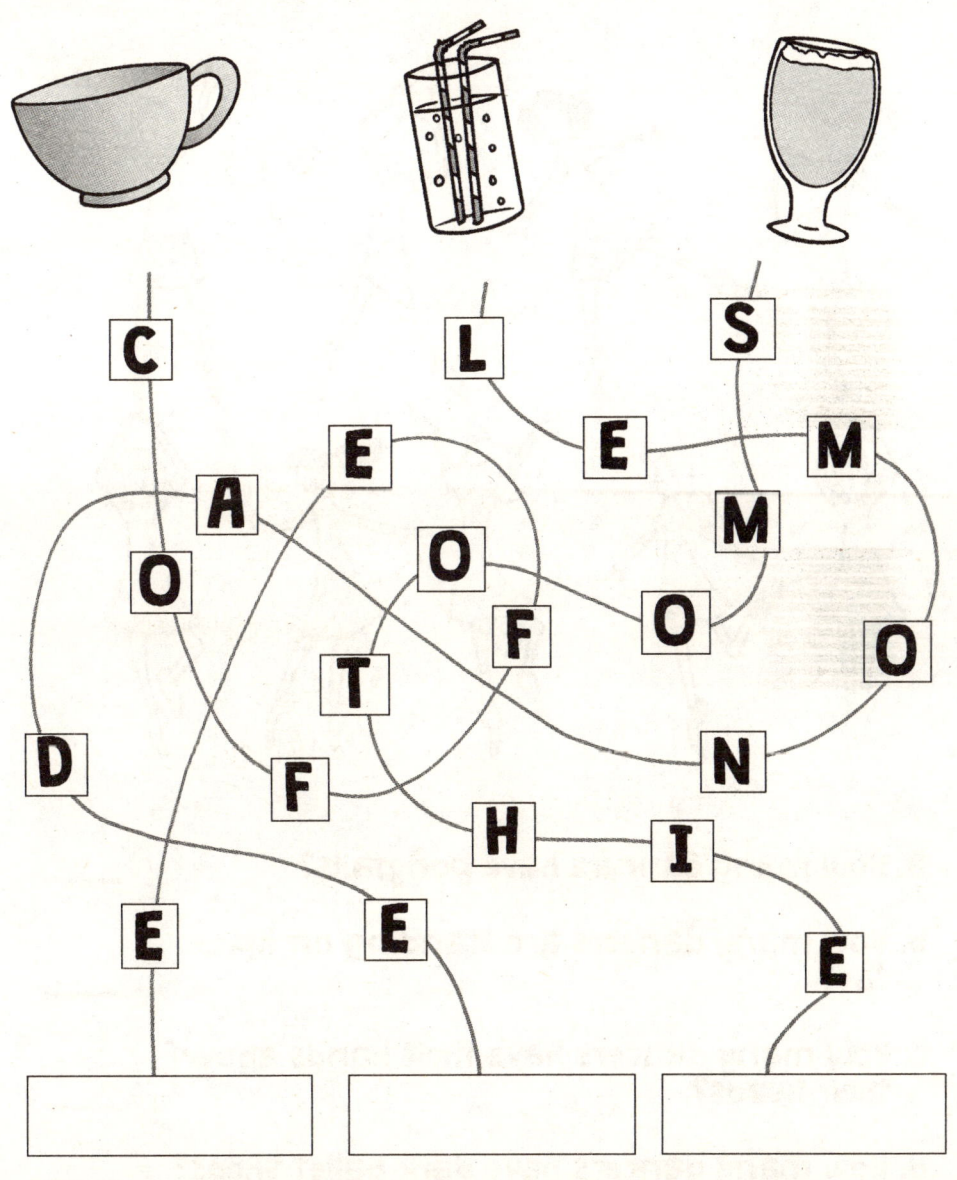

207. At the ballet

These dancers are all rehearsing for a big show. Study them carefully and then answer the questions below.

a. How many dancers have ponytails? ____

b. How many dancers are standing on tip toe? ____

c. How many dancers have their hands above their heads? ____

d. How many dancers have dark ballet shoes? ____

e. How many dancers are wearing leggings? ____

208. I have two eyes but not a tail. I swim around but am not a whale. My legs are long, but I can't walk. My head is large, but I can't talk. What am I?

209. Why are sea creatures with shells not fun to be with?

210. What runs into the ocean but stays in its bed the whole time?

Answers on pages 237-238

211. The school librarian sets her class a challenge. "Let's say there is a banknote hidden in this library. If any of you can find it, then you may keep it as a prize. The money is slotted between pages 57 and 58 of a nonfiction title." Half of the class jump up and start pulling books off the shelves. The other half don't even leave their chairs. Why not?

212. Brutus the dog was born in 5 BCE and died exactly ten years later. In what year did he die?

213. Which word has the most letters in it?

214. Count to 55

There are 5 pairs of numbers that add up to 55 in the grid. Can you circle them?

50	5	20	8	11
12	5	40	15	5
6	20	30	25	5
35	20	8	15	15
7	15	5	37	18

Answers on page 238

215. Who's this?

Follow the start arrow and the compass clues to reveal this boy's name.

3 squares East	___
2 squares North	___
2 squares West	___
4 squares North	___
6 squares East	___

N
W — E
S

- - - - - - -

E	Q	T	U	H	K	S
S	V	M	S	L	P	T
H	Q	N	K	Q	W	U
D	Y	J	L	S	B	L
M	J	A	C	D	J	C
K	O	X	H	K	B	Q
H	P	J	E	X	Q	H

START →

216. Mystery Word

Each line of this puzzle is a clue to a different letter. Can you discover the hidden word?

My first begins speech but also ends books.
My second is in sees but never in looks.
My third is in nice and also in not.
My fourth is a drink you can make in a pot.
My fifth is the same as my second ... that's handy!
My sixth's in vanilla and bonbon and candy.
My seventh appears in country, scene, and place.
My eighth's at the end of the tale and the race.
My whole can be written or spoken by any,
but my beginning and end are
forgotten by many.
What am I?

S
e
n
T
e
n
C
e

217. What do pixies learn first at school?

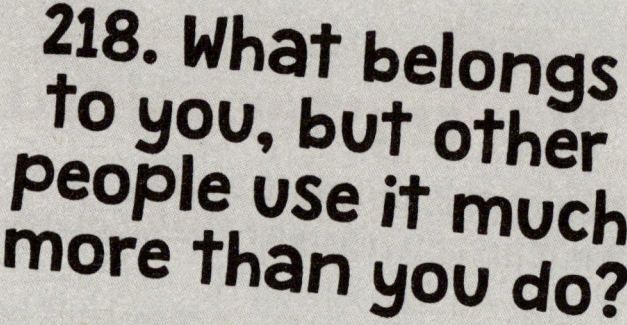

218. What belongs to you, but other people use it much more than you do?

219. You have to poke me in the eye to get me to do what you want. I often live in a box, but you'd never find me in a haystack. What am I?

220. Toby's mother went to the hospital to have her appendix removed. His sister went to the hospital a month later to have her tonsils taken out. A week after that, Toby needed a growth from his head removed. Why didn't he go to the hospital?

221. Snap, snap!

Which reptile is on the prowl? Follow the trail and write down every second letter to find out.

S C P R Z O N C R O J D U I K L Q E B

‾‾ ‾‾ ‾‾ ‾‾ ‾‾ ‾‾ ‾‾ ‾‾ ‾‾ ‾‾

Answers on page 239

222. Letter puzzle

In this grid, there are 4 sets of 3 letters
that sit next to each other in the alphabet.
Can you circle them?

Q	M	N	O	W
P	D	E	F	C
R	I	G	A	V
S	T	U	H	Y
X	B	J	K	L

124

Answers on page 239

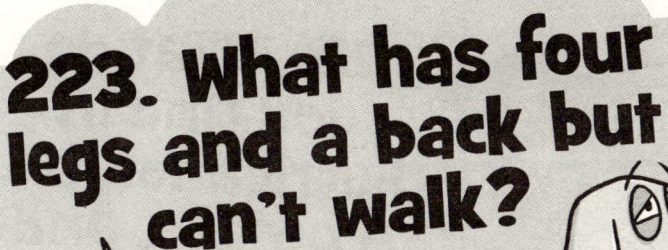

223. What has four legs and a back but can't walk?

224. I am buried in wood from one end to the other, but my head is on show while I hold things together. Do you know what I am?

225. I am very good at what I do. I do my job whenever you want, and I'm always on time, but nobody likes me. What am I?

226. What do you find in hurricanes, on a potato, and on the farmer that grows the second and sees the first coming?

227. A farmer was hard at work building a fence, when a tiny thing stopped her. Although she didn't want it, she kept on looking for it. Eventually, she took it home with her because she couldn't find it. What was it?

228. What does a dog do that a person steps into?

229. Money-go-round

Cross out 4 items of clothing, 4 types of pets, and 4 types of bikes in the selection below. What connects the remaining words?

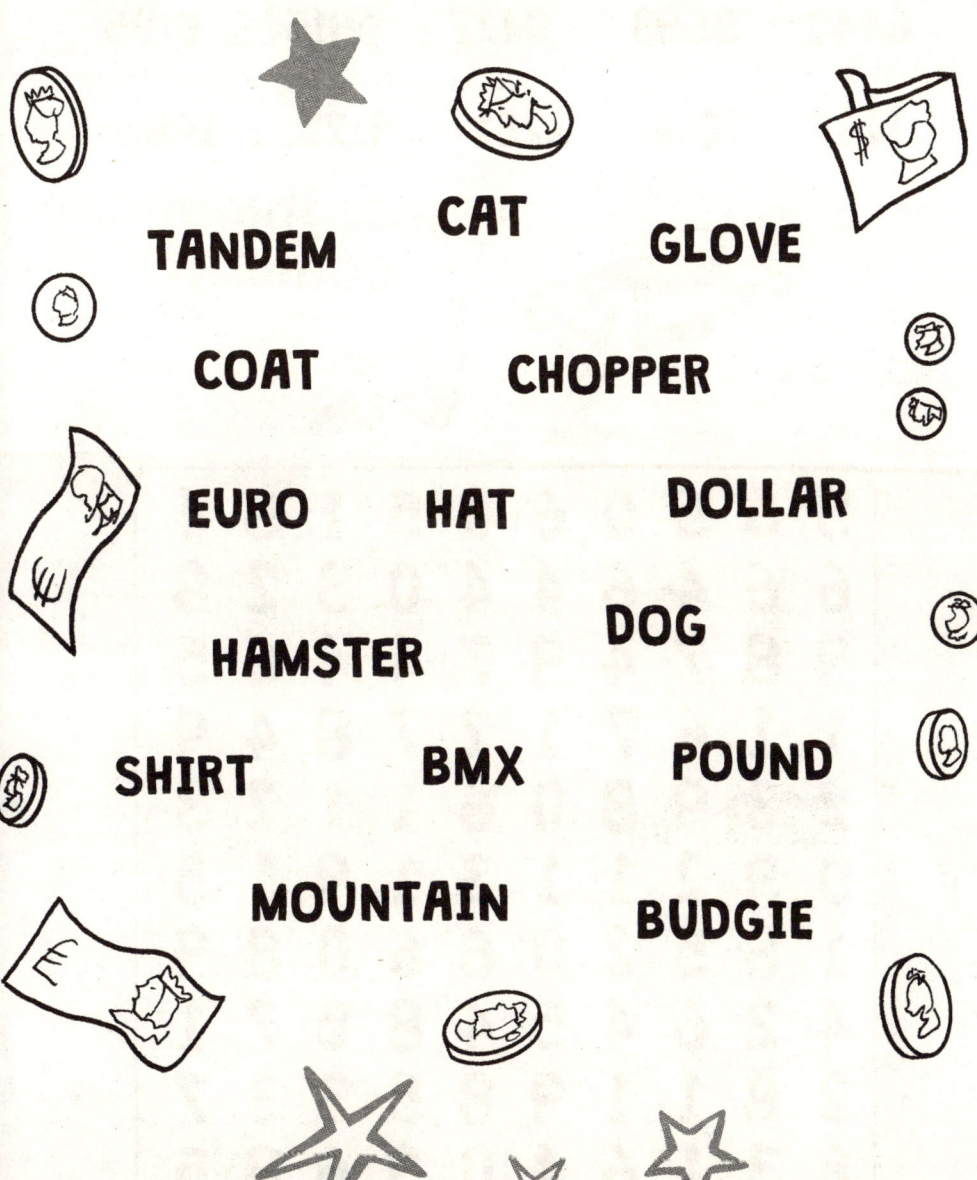

TANDEM   CAT   GLOVE

COAT   CHOPPER

EURO   HAT   DOLLAR

DOG

HAMSTER

SHIRT   BMX   POUND

MOUNTAIN   BUDGIE

230. Nutty numbers

Find the number sequences hidden in the grid. Look up, down, across, and diagonally.

6440	8593	0471	1915	0105
1167	2014	2251	9175	1985

```
5 6 5 0 6 3 5 1 8 4
6 6 4 6 4 4 0 3 2 8
9 8 7 4 9 7 4 4 6 5
1 1 6 7 1 2 7 8 4 9
2 3 9 8 0 6 1 1 2 3
0 9 2 1 1 3 1 9 1 5
1 8 5 2 0 6 6 0 8 9
4 2 6 4 5 4 8 5 7 1
2 8 1 1 9 8 5 3 3 7
8 3 1 6 4 0 9 6 8 5
```

231. Mystery Word

Each line of this puzzle is a clue to a letter. Can you discover the hidden word?

My first is in goats and also in sheep.
My second's in paw but isn't in weep.
My third is in wood but isn't in grow.
My fourth's just the same as my third, don't you know.
My fifth is in bleated and cluck and in squealed.
My sixth is in stable and meadow and field.
My whole is an item you need for a horse, though the horse is quite happy without one, of course!

232. Read this riddle to a friend out loud: "There are 20 sick sheep in a field, and six of them have to be taken to the vet. How many are left?"

Answers on page 240

233. A frog sits on a lily pad in the middle of a circular pond. He is 40 feet from the edge. His first jump takes him to a lily pad 20 feet away. After his first jump, he always jumps half the distance of his previous jump. How many jumps must he make to reach dry land?

234. I have a bushy tail but do not sweep.
I stay awake while you're asleep.
Just like a wolf, my fur is brown.
I'm totally wild but live in town.
What am I?

235. How do you describe an exhausted frog?

236. Fruit bowl

Follow the trails to spell out three types of fruit. Write the answers in the boxes.

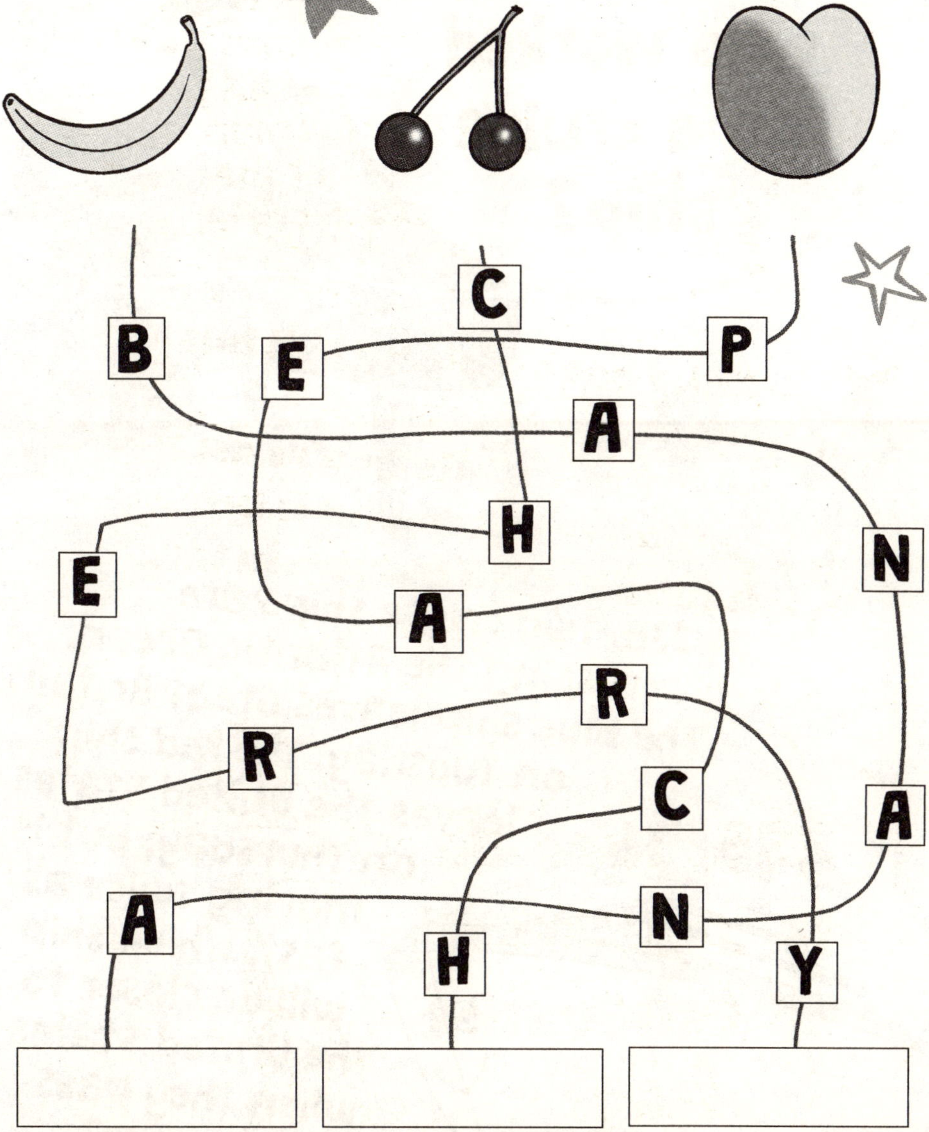

B E C P

A

E H

A

R

R

N

A

E

A H N C Y

237. What happened to the pianist who worked on a cruise ship?

238. Two cruise ships are crossing the Atlantic Ocean. The blue ship leaves Great Britain on Tuesday. The red ship leaves the United States on Thursday, but is moving twice as fast. Which ship will be closer to the United States when they pass each other?

239. Total numbers

Fill in the grid so that each row, column, and mini-square contains a number from 1 to 4.

4			
			2
2		1	4
	4		

240. Lost and found

Break the code to find out who has lost this sheep.

$$\overline{18}\ \overline{15}\ \overline{26}\ \overline{26}\ \overline{18}\ \overline{11}\quad \overline{8}\ \overline{21}\quad \overline{22}\ \overline{11}\ \overline{11}\ \overline{22}$$

Answers on page 241

241. Which of these is the odd one out? Banana, orange, egg, pistachio, apple, avocado.

242. I wear a cap but have no head;
Pick the wrong one, and you might be dead.
I stand up straight but have no feet;
Pick the right one, and I'm good to eat.

243. Time for some arithmetic! If it takes four minutes to boil an egg, how long will it take to boil 12 eggs?

244. If an ice cream sundae with sauce costs $2.10, and the sundae costs $2 more than the sauce, how much does a sundae without sauce cost?

245. How many times does the letter "f" appear in this sentence: "Friends will not feel full of food after eating, if they feel that your food is merely a trifle!"

246. Flower pots

These flowers are lined up to be judged in a flower show. Study them carefully and answer the questions below.

a. How many flowers have five petals? ____

b. How many flowerpots have stripes? ____

c. How many flowerpots have zig zags? ____

d. How many flowers have four petals? ____

e. How many flowerpots have two flowers? ____

247. Count to 60

There are 5 pairs of numbers that add up to 60 in the grid. Can you circle them?

30	8	20	30	30
10	40	20	9	5
50	10	30	10	8
20	20	6	45	15
42	18	8	20	10

Answers on page 242

248. Take away

Follow the start arrow and the compass clues to find out what type of fast food the woman is delivering.

6 squares West   ___

2 squares North   ___

4 squares East   ___

4 squares North   ___

5 squares West   ___

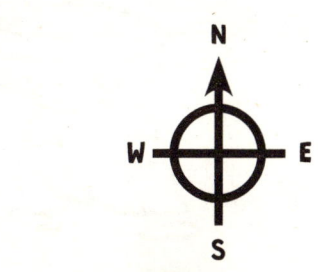

_ _ _ _ _

A	D	V	J	H	Z	Y
S	E	L	N	O	Y	D
X	C	U	A	I	E	T
B	N	Q	W	L	L	J
N	I	W	I	P	Z	K
I	X	T	U	S	B	Q
H	P	O	G	T	K	Q

START ←

249. Funky figures

Fill in the grid so that each row, column, and mini-square contains a number from 1 to 4.

4			
	3	4	
	4	3	
	1		4

Answers on page 242

250. Which fast food gets hotter when it sounds colder?

251. Here's a rhyme to test your head. We'll call it "The Tale of Ruby Red." A stick in her top, A pit in her middle, I'll give you a prize If you answer this riddle.

252. How many peas are there in a pod?

253. All shook up!

Follow the trail and write down every second letter to find a type of drink.

O M D I W L V K M S L H U A F K Q E Z

__ __ __ __ __ __ __ __ __

Answers on page 242

254. Where in America?

Break the code to find a state in the U.S. It is nicknamed "The Golden State" because lots of gold has been found there.

<u>   </u> <u>   </u> <u>   </u> <u>   </u> <u>   </u> <u>   </u> <u>   </u> <u>   </u> <u>   </u> <u>   </u>
 9   7   18   15   12   21   24   20   15   7

255. A bridge is 3 miles long and strong enough to hold exactly 22,000 pounds but no more. A loaded truck that weighs exactly 21,999 pounds drives onto the bridge. In the middle, a sparrow that weighs 5 ounces lands on the truck, yet the bridge doesn't collapse. How could this be?

256. Most animals grow up. Which animals grow down?

257. How did the farmer find his lost daughter?

258. Alphabetical

In this grid, there are 4 sets of 3 letters
that sit next to each other in the alphabet.
Can you circle them?

U	N	P	Z	T
B	C	D	G	M
L	H	I	J	O
Q	R	S	V	K
E	W	X	Y	F

Answers on page 243

259. Number crunching

Find the number sequences hidden in the grid. Look up, down, across, and diagonally.

4502	9407	4682	6093	6953
2152	8534	4218	3142	3329

```
5 4 7 9 4 0 7 4 7 1
9 5 5 0 7 1 8 6 5 0
6 3 3 0 6 9 2 8 8 6
6 0 9 3 2 5 4 2 3 9
9 8 6 5 8 3 7 3 4 4
5 2 2 4 5 6 2 1 9 2
3 5 1 8 8 4 1 4 2 1
1 9 5 3 3 2 9 2 5 8
0 3 2 1 4 8 3 5 1 3
4 0 3 6 1 0 8 9 0 6
```

260. A polar bear walks 3 miles north and then 2 miles south. He ends up 5 miles from his starting point. How can that be?

261. What kind of socks do polar bears wear?

262. Why do seagulls live by the sea?

263. Going places

Follow the trail and write down every second letter to find a type of transport.

‗‗ ‗‗ ‗‗ ‗‗ ‗‗ ‗‗ ‗‗ ‗‗ ‗‗ ‗‗

Answers on page 244

264. Woody walk

Cross out 4 types of weather, 4 cities, and 4 types of tools in the selection below. What connects the remaining words?

SUNSHINE

DRILL

LONDON

SNOW

AX

WIND

NEW YORK

HAMMER

TOKYO

SCREWDRIVER

OAK

PINE

MOSCOW

BEECH

RAIN

265. Something fishy

Study the fish in the aquarium and answer the questions below.

a. How many fish are striped? ____

b. How many fish have spots? ____

c. How many fish are long and thin? ____

d. How many fish are blowing bubbles? ____

e. How many fish have big tails? ____

150

266. Over the sea

Break the code to find a type of noisy seabird.

$\overline{25}$ $\overline{11}$ $\overline{7}$ $\overline{13}$ $\overline{18}$ $\overline{18}$

267. What is two feet long but can be all different sizes?

268. What is being described here?
When I am full, I can point the way, but when I am empty, I lie still. I keep you warm on a snowy day, but I'm useless when it's sunny.

269. What has a neck but no head, with two arms but no hands?

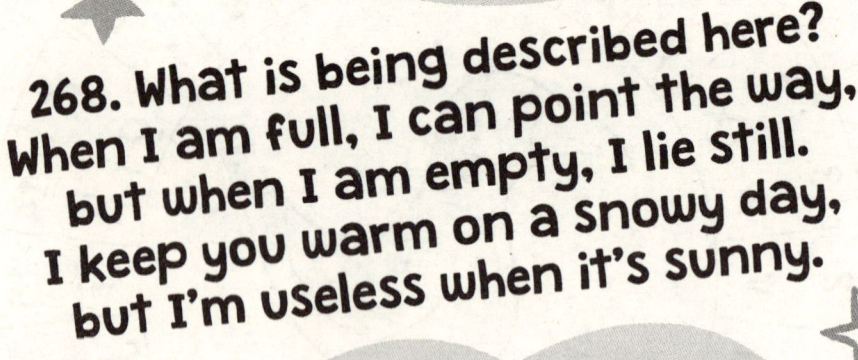

270. What's the weather?

Follow the trails to spell out three types of weather. Write the answers in the boxes.

271. What did the shoes say to the hat before setting out on a walk?

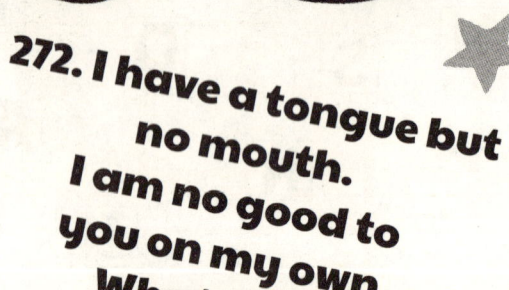

272. I have a tongue but no mouth. I am no good to you on my own. What am I?

273. When is a coat no use to keep out the cold?

154

Answers on pages 244-245

274. Number grids

Fill in the grid so that each row, column, and mini-square contains a number from 1 to 4.

		1	2
2			
			4
4	3		

275. Secret numbers

Find the number sequences hidden in the grid. Look up, down, across, and diagonally.

2163	6350	8416	2580	5559
6966	0572	3433	8620	7581

```
2 1 6 3 0 1 3 4 3 3
6 5 9 1 1 8 5 5 9 6
3 8 5 4 8 7 7 8 5 9
5 6 3 5 7 6 9 6 1 7
0 3 4 6 9 5 6 3 4 5
8 4 1 6 3 9 1 4 8 8
8 8 2 4 6 2 0 9 6 1
3 2 5 7 4 0 5 5 2 4
7 0 8 1 2 4 7 1 0 2
1 4 0 2 5 1 2 0 8 3
```

276. Secret letters

In this grid, there are 4 sets of 3 letters that sit next to each other in the alphabet. Can you circle them?

H	C	E	F	G
W	B	S	X	J
T	U	V	R	D
A	K	L	M	I
Y	Q	N	O	P

277. What number?

Find the number sequences hidden in the grid. Look up, down, across, and diagonally.

5926   6320   4185   9978   7273

9347   6246   3492   9360   9399

```
1 3 1 0 6 3 2 0 5 4
5 5 8 1 9 7 4 1 8 5
8 9 9 9 7 6 5 6 3 6
9 6 3 8 8 5 8 9 4 9
3 7 8 6 2 8 6 8 9 0
4 8 2 3 4 1 9 3 2 2
7 1 7 7 6 9 3 6 0 4
1 5 0 5 3 1 1 7 1 7
6 4 1 4 8 6 4 5 4 1
9 3 9 9 5 2 0 1 8 9
```

Answers on page 246

278. Yummy snacks

Cross out 4 months of the year, 4 swimming strokes, and 4 rivers in the selection below. What connects the remaining words?

CRAWL

THAMES

JANUARY

PEAR

BREASTSTROKE

JUNE

APRIL

AMAZON

NILE

BACKSTROKE

MISSISSIPPI

MAY

BUTTERFLY

BANANA

APPLE

279. Funny faces

This class is ready for their school picture. Look at them closely and answer the questions below.

a. How many faces are happy? ____

b. How many faces are sad? ____

c. How many faces have tongues sticking out? ____

d. How many faces are winking? ____

e. How many faces are asleep? ____

280. Where does the biggest herd of pigs live?

281. Mystery Word

Each line of this puzzle is a clue to a letter. Can you discover the hidden word?

My first is in chew and also in cud.
My second's in goad but isn't in good.
My third and my fourth are letters the same,
found in cart and in tractor, in stock
and in train.
My fifth is in lamb and in billy but not beef.
My last is in sleep and rest and relief.
My whole can be found on a farm, big or small.
Even when you can't see me, you'll
still know my call.

Answers on page 246

282. What five-letter word becomes shorter when you add two letters to it?

283. What has a head and a tail but no legs?

284. Rosie's mother has three daughters. She has chosen their names very carefully. The oldest is April and the middle one is May. What did she name the youngest one?

285. Where am I from?

Nick, Eva, and Harry are all from different countries. Follow the trails to find out which ones.

286. Hard cheese

This mouse has managed to swipe a nice, big lump of cheese. Follow the start arrow and the compass clues to find out what type it is.

5 squares East — C

1 square North — H

4 squares West — E

2 squares North — D

6 squares East — D

3 squares North — A

6 squares West — R

C H E D D A R

R	S	Z	N	L	T	A
Q	A	X	W	S	D	V
B	F	T	Y	H	K	M
D	U	L	Q	Z	G	D
Y	K	P	W	E	B	K
E	R	Y	J	H	S	P
W	G	J	A	C	L	B

START →

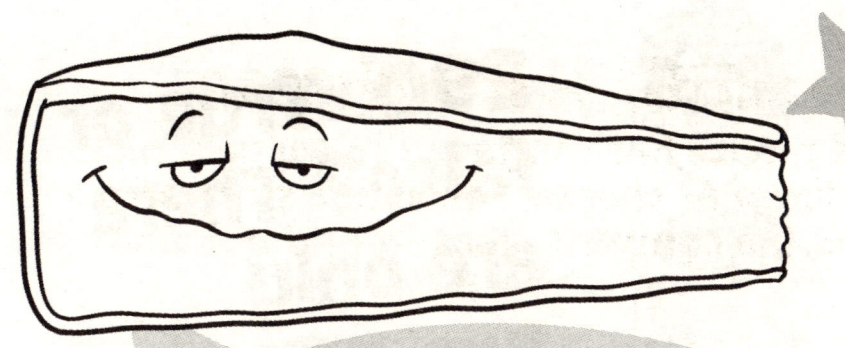

**287. I have some cheese.
He has some cheese, too,
and so does she.
They are all the same type of
cheese. What type is that?**

**288. Let us find the hidden vegetable,
Speak aloud to figure it out.
When we've found the
hidden vegetable,
Let us give a happy shout.**

289. What type of cheese is made backward?

290. True or false? There are only two "F"s in "Farmer Fuffle."

291. A chestnut tree has an average of 6 branches, with 12 twigs on each branch and 24 nuts on each twig. How many acorns are there on one tree?

292. What is all ears and says "shhhh" but doesn't listen to a word you say?

293. Count to 70

There are 5 pairs of numbers that add up to 70 in the grid. Can you circle them?

35	35	20	20	9
15	40	30	10	20
7	19	10	45	25
11	55	15	8	10
6	30	8	60	10

Answers on page 247

294. At the bakers

Break the code to find what kind of bread the baker has made this morning.

$\overline{}$ $\overline{}$ $\overline{}$ $\overline{}$ $\overline{}$ $\overline{}$ $\overline{}$ $\overline{}$
8   7   13   1   11   26   26   11

Answers on page 247

295. Chain letters

In this grid, there are 4 sets of 3 letters that sit next to each other in the alphabet. Can you circle them?

Y	C	D	E	T
G	X	O	P	Q
F	N	L	Z	H
I	J	K	A	S
B	U	V	W	M

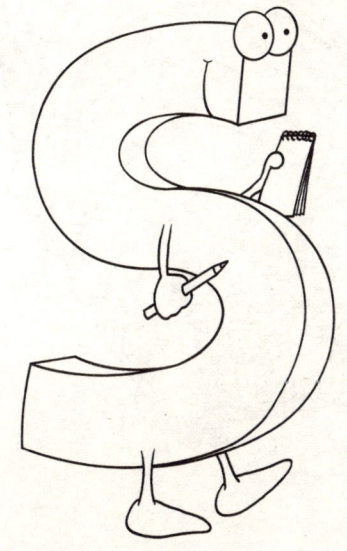

296. Farmer Jake was on one side of the river, and his trusty dog, Elmer, was on the other side. There was no bridge or boat. The farmer whistled to Elmer and shouted, "Here boy! Come on!" Elmer crossed the river, and they both walked back to the farmhouse. However, Elmer didn't get wet. How can that be?

297. What always sleeps with its shoes on?

298. Tricky numbers

Fill in the grid so that each row, column, and mini-square contains a number from 1 to 4.

4			
		4	
	1	2	
2			3

299. When is a swan the same as corn?

300. What has two heads and one tail, and walks on four legs?

301. I live in the river but don't have any fins. If you canoe past, I might tip you in. When it looks like I'm bored, I'm actually cross. Even the crocodiles know I'm the boss!

302. In space

Follow the trail and write down every second letter to find a distant giant planet.

-- -- -- -- -- -- --

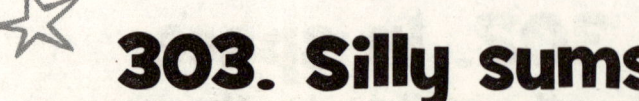

303. Silly sums

Find the number sequences hidden in the grid. Look up, down, across, and diagonally.

1103	7306	6886	1548	0359
0292	2869	5275	5498	8254

```
4 5 0 2 9 2 1 1 0 3
2 2 2 4 4 1 9 7 1 5
8 6 4 7 2 8 3 4 5 2
6 8 9 1 5 6 8 8 6 9
9 1 5 4 8 4 6 5 8 8
5 2 8 5 6 9 5 3 3 2
0 4 5 0 3 5 9 9 5 5
1 7 9 6 7 3 0 6 9 4
5 2 6 8 1 7 5 4 2 7
7 7 3 0 2 0 1 8 4 3
```

Answers on pages 248-249

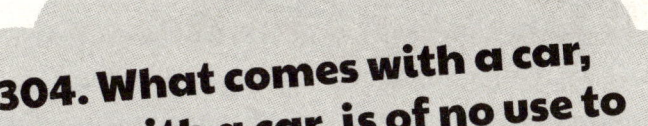

304. What comes with a car, goes with a car, is of no use to the car, but the car cannot go without it?

305. What travel mode has eight wheels but can only carry one passenger?

306. What has six wheels and flies?

307. How do you get down from a donkey?

308. What animal can jump higher than an elephant?

309. What animal wears more in the summer than it does in the winter?

310. What's a foot?

Cross out 4 baby animals, 4 things to do with Christmas, and 4 circus acts in the selection below. What connects the remaining words?

 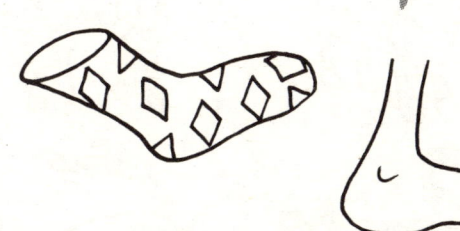

SHOE

LAMB   **CLOWN**   **KITTEN**

FOAL   **ACROBAT**

MISTLETOE

                        PRESENT

FIRE-EATER   **BOOT**

                        SANTA

       JUGGLER

SLEIGH

                        PUPPY

   SNEAKER

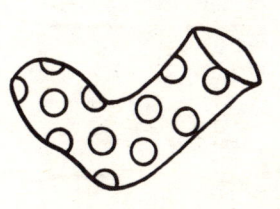   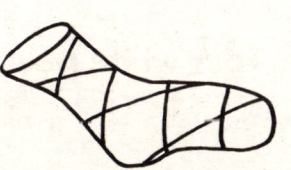   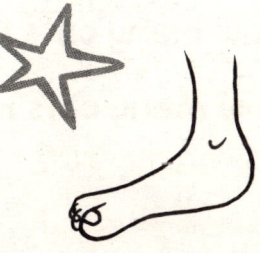

Answers on page 249

311. Cat show

These pretty kitties are all lined up for judging. Look at them carefully and answer the questions below.

a. How many cats have stripes? ____

b. How many cats have two black paws? ____

c. How many cats have collars? ____

d. How many cats have no whiskers? ____

e. How many cats have four white paws? ____

Answers on page 249

312. Mystery Word

Each line of this puzzle is a clue to a letter. Can you discover the hidden word?

My first is in large and also in big,
My second's in wait but isn't in twig.
My third is in car, and in ride,
and in truck.
My fourth is in sat but isn't in stuck.
My fifth is in gas but isn't in tanks.
My sixth is in creaks but isn't in cranks.
Figure out the letters, and write
each one down:
My whole can be found
by a house or in town.

313. Which burns longer, a short, fat candle or a tall, thin one?

179

314. A cowboy rides into town on Friday, stays for two days, and leaves on Friday. How can that be?

315. I am a seven-letter word, but if you take away four letters, only one is left. I'm a real beast ... you might even say I'm the queen! Who am I?

316. What does a buffalo say to her son when he leaves for school?

317. Arty party

Follow the trails to spell out three shades of the pencil, paintbrush, and paint tube. Write the answers in the boxes.

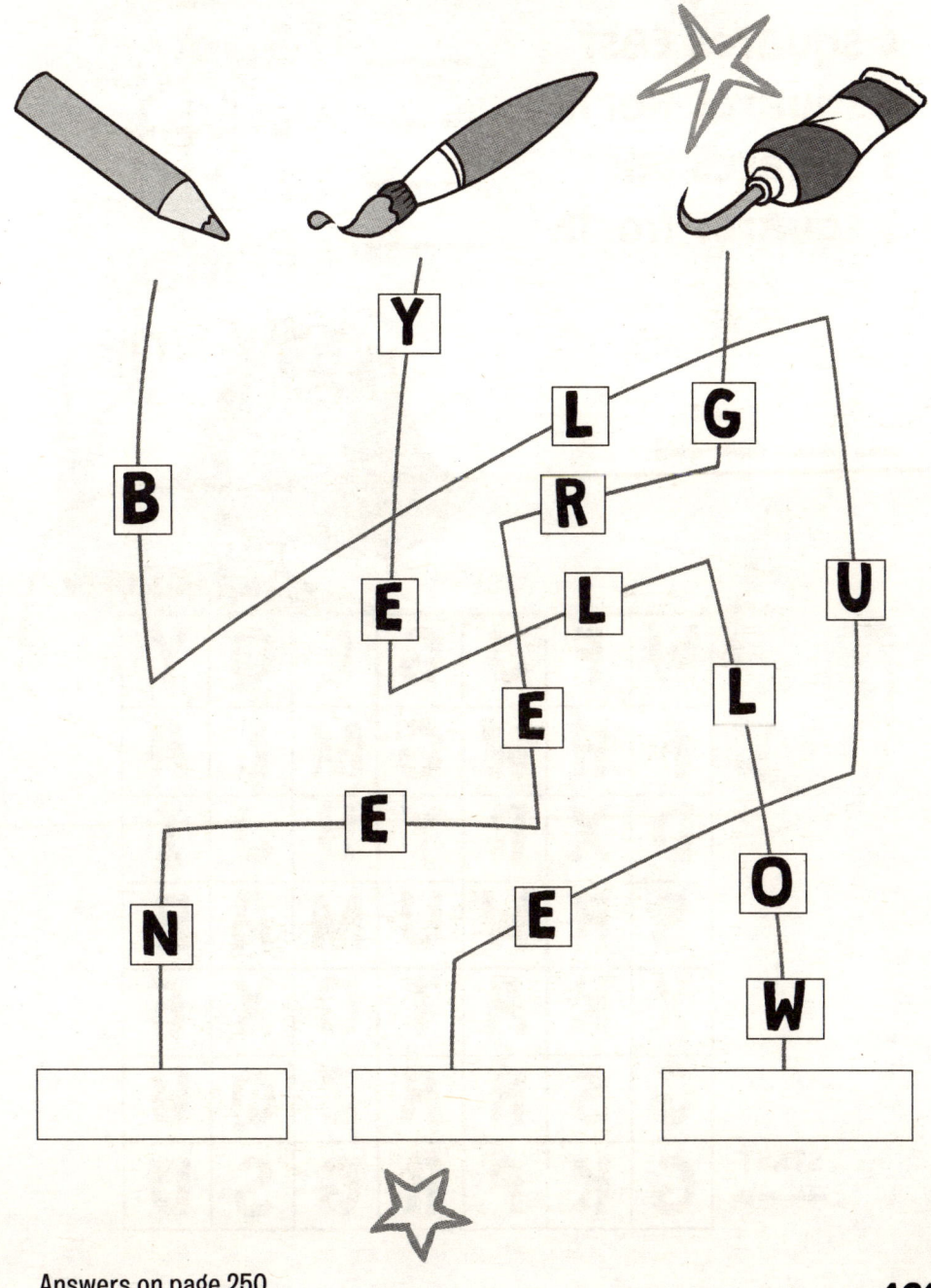

318. Shiny stone

Follow the start arrow and the compass clues to find what Tina's birthstone is.

4 squares East   ___
3 squares North   ___
3 squares East   ___
3 squares North   ___

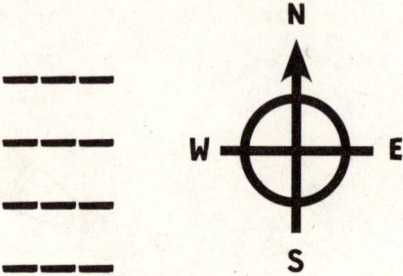

_ _ _ _

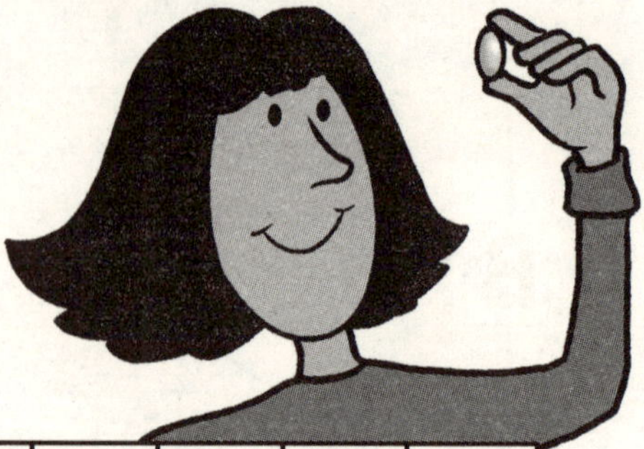

W	F	J	G	E	Q	Y
F	H	W	G	M	L	A
D	X	R	Y	H	J	I
S	R	W	U	M	A	B
X	K	A	T	O	X	E
G	S	R	A	Z	Q	H
G	K	P	R	G	S	D

START →

Answers on page 250

319. If you screw a light bulb into a socket by turning the bulb clockwise with your right hand, which way would you turn the socket with your left hand in order to unscrew it, while holding the bulb still?

320. What has rivers but no water, cities but no people, and forests but no trees?

321. What is always hot, even if you keep it in the refrigerator?

322. Pussy cat

Break the code to find a type of fluffy cat.

(wheel cipher: 6=z, 7=a, 8=b, 9=c, 10=d, 11=e, 12=f, 13=g, 14=h, 15=i, 16=j, 17=k, 18=l, 19=m, 20=n, 21=o, 22=p, 23=q, 24=r, 25=s, 26=t, 1=u, 2=v, 3=w, 4=x, 5=y)

<u>22</u> <u>11</u> <u>24</u> <u>25</u> <u>15</u> <u>7</u> <u>20</u>

184

Answers on page 250

323. A mother has two sons who share a birthday and were born in the same year, but they are not twins. How could this happen?

324. How can you tell that birthdays are good for you?

325. What has a face and two hands but no arms or legs?

326. What gets bigger the more you take away from it?

327. In the warm months, I wear green, both during the day and at night. As it cools, I wear yellow, but during winter, I wear white. What am I?

328. The grand old nag gallops with great delight, then it grazes on grass and sleeps at night. He's a strong friend for the farmer and me; now, how many times did you count "g"?

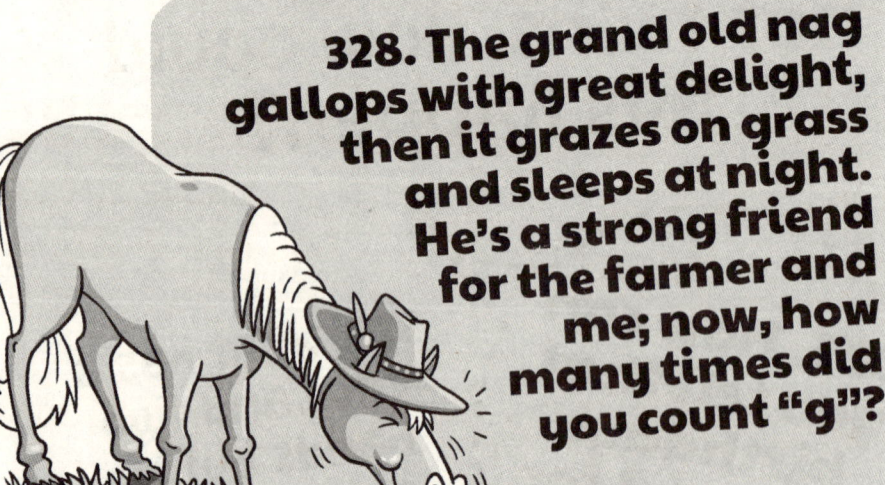

329. Count to 80

There are 5 pairs of numbers that add up to 80 in the grid. Can you circle them?

40	40	20	15	7
20	5	70	10	20
10	60	20	20	10
10	20	50	30	9
65	15	25	15	10

330. Funny felines

Cross out 4 flowers, 4 types of boats, and 4 fast foods in the selection below. What connects the remaining words?

TULIP

YACHT

BURGER

TUG

ROSE

KEBAB

HOT DOG

PERSIAN

SIAMESE

LILY

BARGE

MANX

DAISY

CHIPS

FERRY

331. Prime numbers

Fill in the grid so that each row, column, and mini-square contains a number from 1 to 4.

3			4
			2
2			
	3	2	1

Answers on page 251

332. Letter grid

In this grid, there are 4 sets of 3 letters that sit next to each other in the alphabet. Can you circle them?

O	P	L	M	N
F	G	H	V	J
K	W	R	S	T
B	E	I	C	Q
X	Y	Z	A	D

Answers on page 252

333. If two birds lay an average of three eggs every day, how many eggs can a peacock lay in three days?

334. What grows even though it is not alive?

335. What can you find in the middle of Uruguay that can't be found anywhere in Brazil or Bolivia?

336. If a red house is made of red bricks, and a brown house is made of brown bricks, what is a green house made of?

337. What goes up and down the stairs without moving?

338. I turn around once;
What is out will not get in.
I turn around again;
What is in will not get out.
What am I?

339. Giant of the sea

Follow the trail and write down every
second letter to find a giant sea creature.

__ __ __ __ __   __ __ __ __ __ __

340. Crack the code

Find the number sequences hidden in the grid. Look up, down, across, and diagonally.

5071   1375   7385   7946   6935

4244   7643   1867   6683   9090

```
5 2 0 1 7 6 1 7 9 0
6 9 1 9 0 9 0 4 6 4
8 6 8 3 9 2 1 2 7 9
2 8 6 7 5 7 2 4 1 0
1 0 9 8 6 8 7 4 8 1
9 1 1 2 3 4 6 9 3 5
5 7 3 2 7 9 3 0 4 3
0 3 7 4 8 3 7 4 9 6
7 6 5 6 2 4 8 8 5 7
3 5 0 7 1 6 1 5 2 2
```

341. Farmer Jennings was in town for the day. He went down Main Street without stopping at the red lights and turned into a street that said "NO ENTRY." A police officer waved as he went past and didn't give him a ticket or even tell him off. Why was that?

342. When is a black dog not a black dog?

343. What do you call an experienced vet?

Answers on pages 252-253

344. Mystery Word

Each line of this puzzle is a clue to a letter. Can you discover the hidden word?

My first is in pasta and soup and in pit.
My second's in biscuit, in whisk, and in whip.
My third is in ice cream, chocolate chip, and cake.
My fourth is in cooking and also in bake.
My fifth is in apple but isn't in pear.
My last is in fare but isn't in flair.
Put all the letters together to spell something that goes with cheese really well.

345. Why do snails never go to hamburger joints?

346. Tasty treat

Cross out 4 shellfish, 4 types of transport, and 4 games in the selection below. What connects the remaining words?

LOBSTER   **TRAIN**   **I-SPY**

CHOC CHIP   **TUTTI FRUTTI**

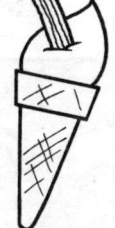

MUSSEL   **SNAP**   **CLAM**

RASPBERRY RIPPLE

CAR

BUS

CRAB   **LUDO**

CHESS   **MOTORBIKE**

Answers on page 253

347. Monster parade

These monsters are dancing at a party. Study them carefully and answer the questions below.

a. How many monsters have four eyes on stalks? ____

b. How many monsters have four arms? ____

c. How many monsters have six arms? ____

d. How many monsters have five eyes on stalks? ____

e. How many monsters have three legs? ____

Answers on page 253

348. Joe is taking his dog for a walk. It doesn't walk in front of him, or behind him, or to one side of him. He isn't carrying it, and of course, it isn't above him or below him. Where is his dog?

349. What do you call a lionfish with no eyes?

350. This case has no hinges, no key, no lid, but golden treasure inside is hid.

351. Letter square

In this grid, there are 3 sets of 4 letters that sit next to each other in the alphabet. Can you circle them?

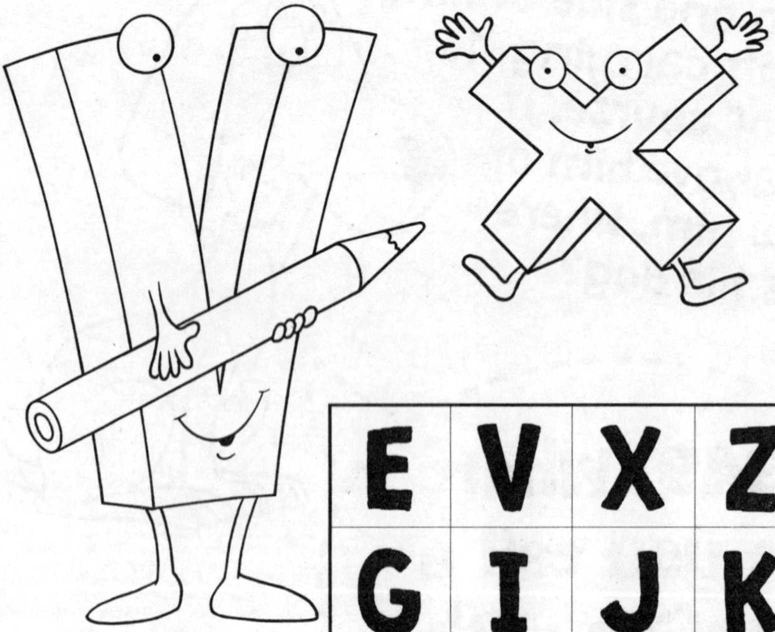

E	V	X	Z	U
G	I	J	K	L
Q	R	S	T	O
M	F	W	Y	N
P	A	B	C	D

Answers on page 254

352. Bird bonanza

Follow the trails to spell out which birds are visiting the garden today. Write the answers in the boxes.

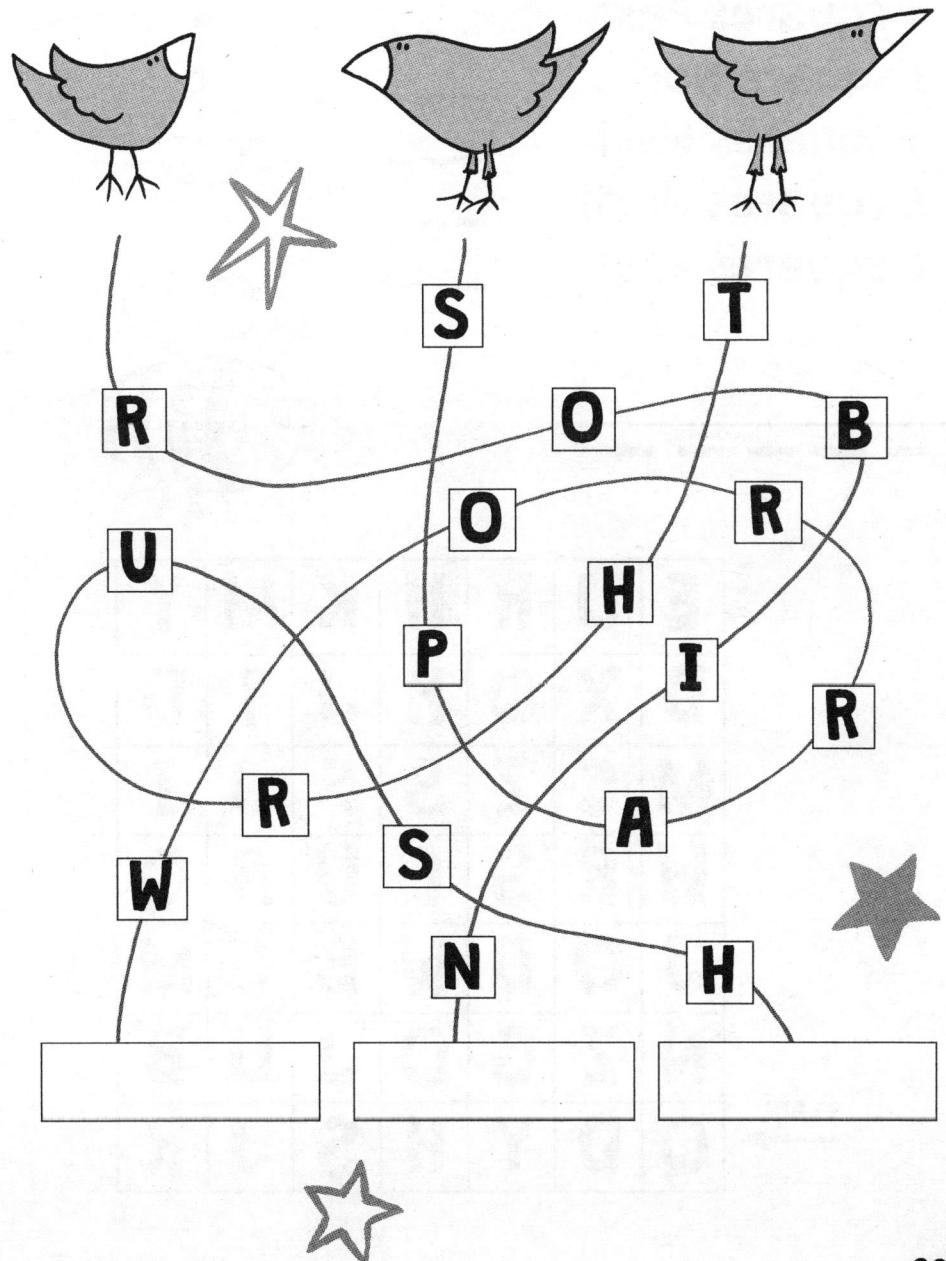

353. Sweet stuff

Follow the start arrow and the compass clues to find out what Boris bee likes to eat.

4 squares East ___

1 square North ___

3 squares West ___

5 squares North ___

6 squares East ___

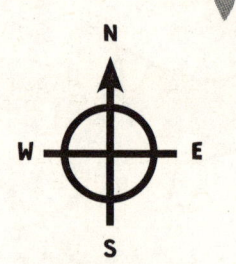

_ _ _ _ _

E	J	R	H	K	M	Y
D	X	Q	H	J	T	D
M	C	Z	S	F	J	I
W	R	S	F	U	A	Q
J	O	D	W	B	C	M
N	Z	G	O	J	U	B
Q	D	Y	H	S	J	R

START →

354. What do a comb, a zipper, and a shark all have in common?

355. What is as round as a frying pan and as deep as a sink, yet all the oceans in the world couldn't fill it up?

356. There is one that has a head without an eye, and there's one that has an eye without a head. You may find the answer if you try; half of what you seek hangs upon the thread.

Answers on page 254

357. Wild cats

Follow the trails to spell out three types of fearsome felines. Write the answers in the boxes.

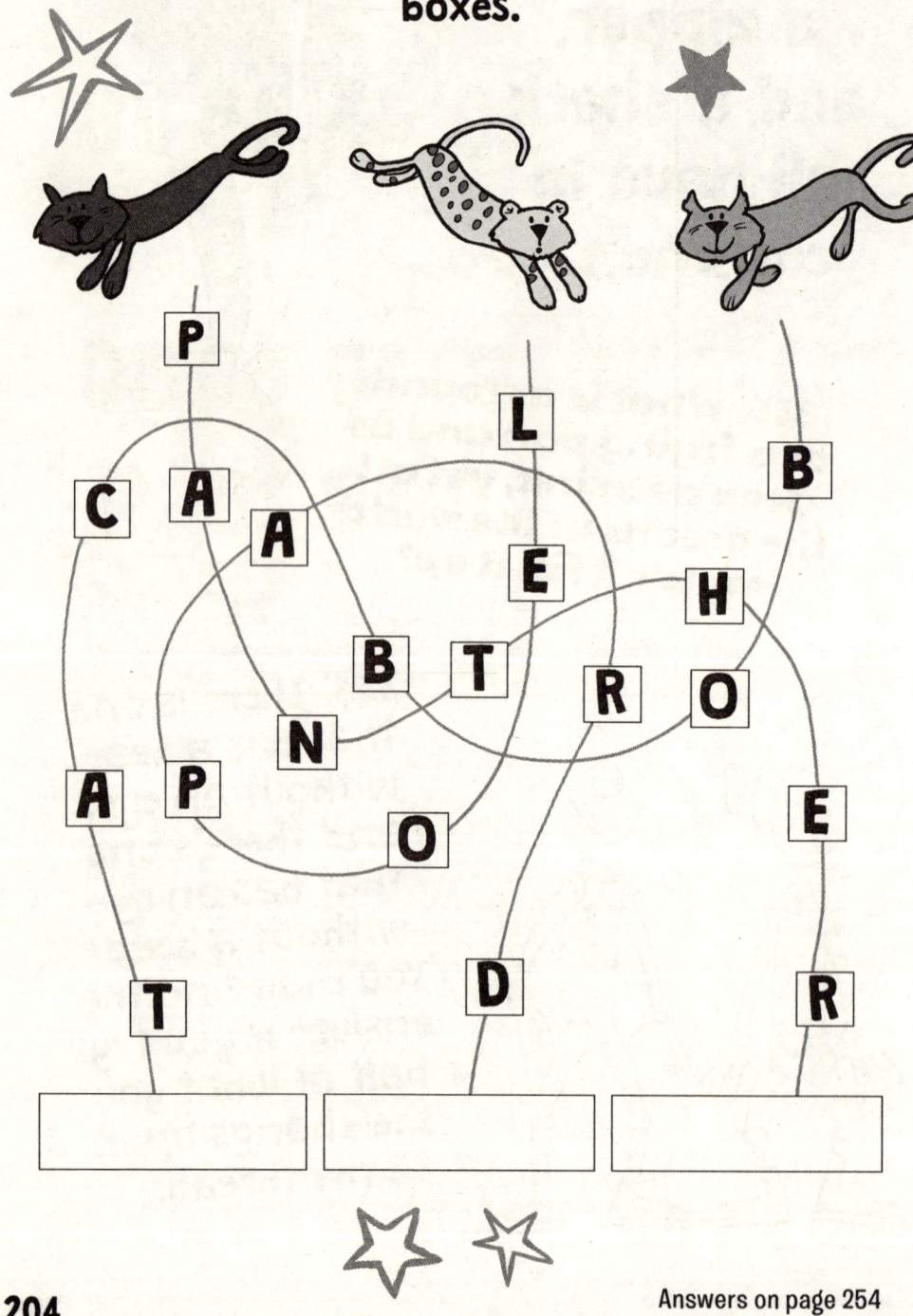

Answers on page 254

358. Count to 90

There are 5 pairs of numbers that add up to 90 in the grid. Can you circle them?

8	20	45	45	20
5	80	10	15	9
30	8	10	60	30
50	40	30	15	9
20	10	65	25	20

359. On your head

Break the code to find a type
of tall hairstyle from the 1960s.

__ __ __ __ __ __ __
8 11 11 14 15 2 11

Answers on page 255

360. A man must cross a river in his boat, taking with him a snake, his pet rat, and a sack of grain.

The boat is only big enough to carry the man and one item at a time.

He can't leave the snake and the rat together, and he can't leave the rat and the grain together.

How does he get everything safely across the river?

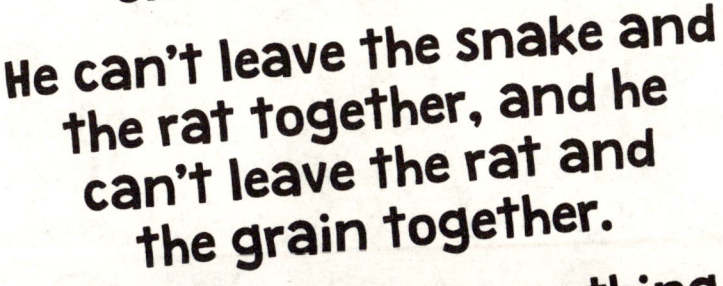

361. Knights, ready!

These knights are all ready for battle. Study them carefully then answer the questions below.

a. How many knights have a feather in their helmet? ____

b. How many knights have a striped shield? ____

c. How many knights have a lance? ____

d. How many knights have a sword? ____

e. How many knights have a flag? ____

362. Which is correct: The yolk of the egg is white, or the yolk of the eggs are white?

363. Farmer Bob was selling some eggs. His first customer said, "I'll buy half your eggs and half an egg more." His second customer said the same thing. His third customer just wanted one egg. Farmer Bob filled their orders without breaking a single egg. How many eggs did Farmer Bob have?

364. When is the best time to buy chicks?

Answers on page 255

365. Sally throws a ball as hard as she can, but it comes straight back to her without bouncing off anything. How did she do it?

366. What is served but never eaten?

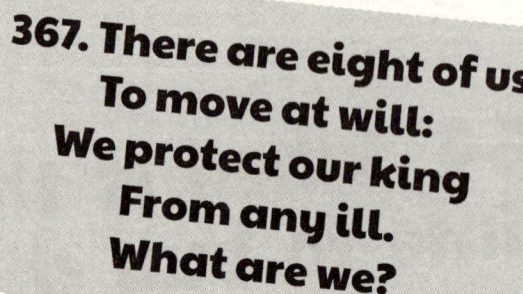

367. There are eight of us
To move at will:
We protect our king
From any ill.
What are we?

368. Four figures

Fill in the grid so that each row, column, and mini-square contains a number from 1 to 4.

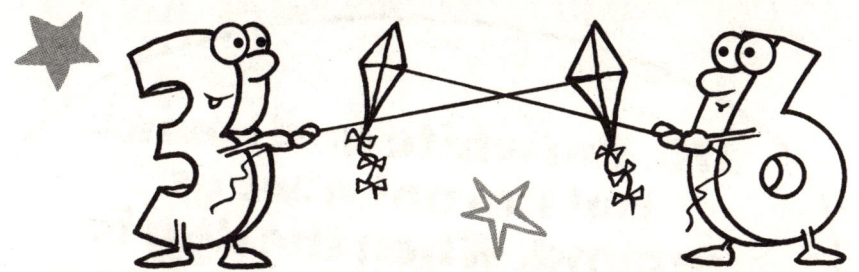

3			1
1			
	1	2	3

369. What has eight legs and flies?

370. I'm white and round, but I'm not always around. When the day is at its brightest, I cannot be found. What am I?

371. Farmer Sally builds three haystacks in her north field and two in her south field. Every week afterward, for five weeks, she doubles the number in the north field and adds two more in the south field. How many haystacks will she have at the end of the harvest if she puts them all together?

372. Spot the dog

Woof! Follow the trails to spell out three types of dogs. Write the answers in the boxes.

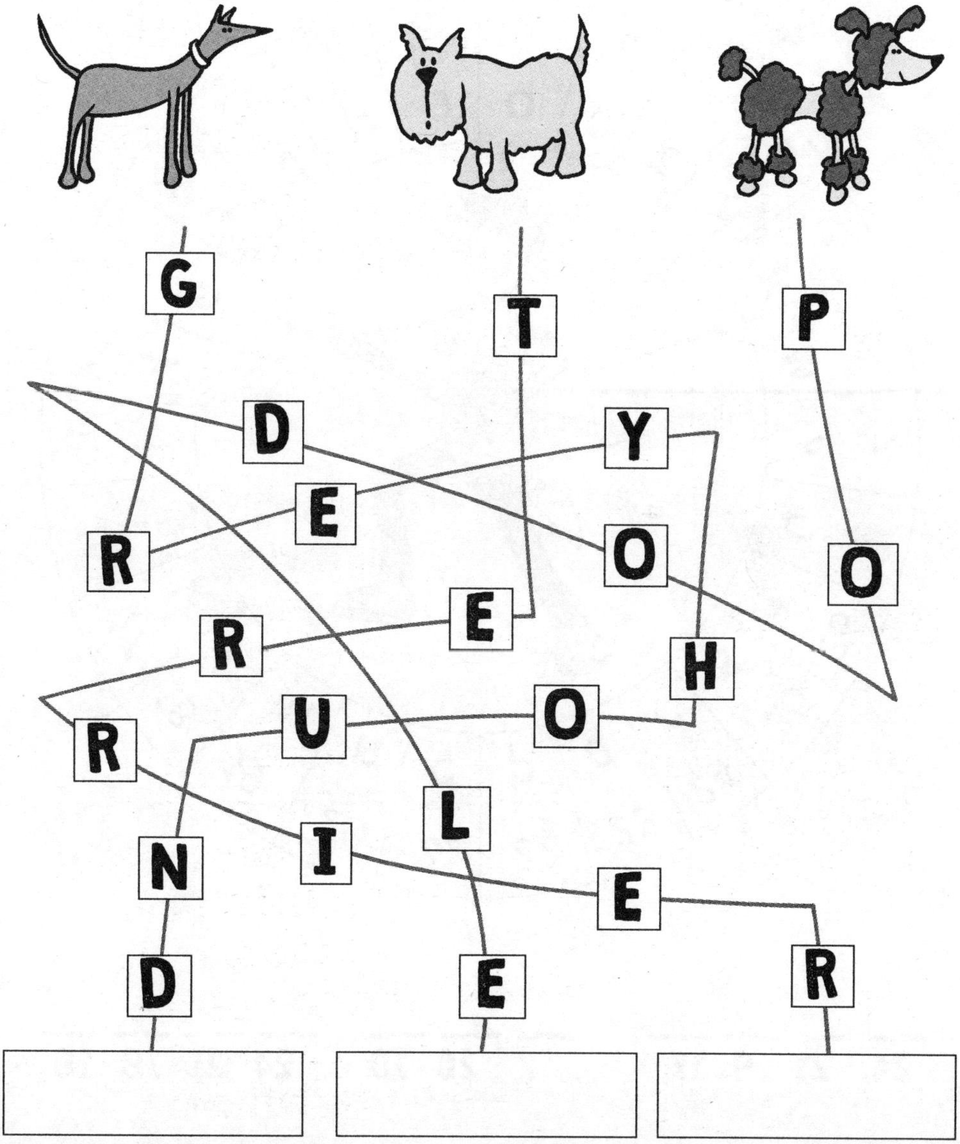

G
T
P
D
Y
E
R
O
R
E
H
R
U
O
N
I
L
E
D
E
R

373. Hear the beat

What kind of music does George like to play? Break the code to find out.

—— —— —— —— —— —— —— —— —— —— ——
24 21 9 17   7 20 10   24 21 18 18

Answers on page 256

374. Number squares

Fill in the grid so that each row, column, and mini-square contains a number from 1 to 4.

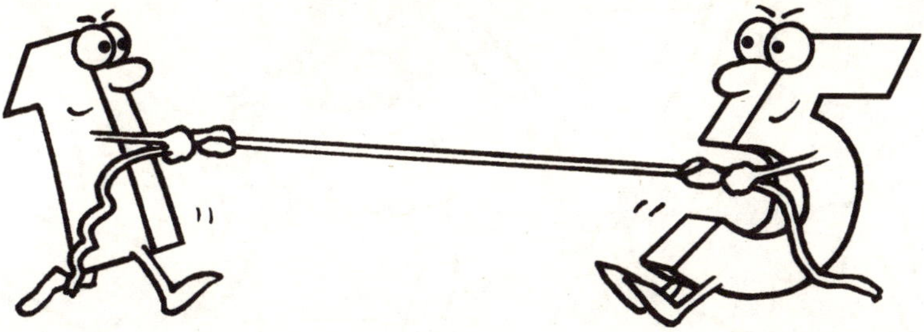

			2
	2		
	3		4
	1	2	

Answers

Pages 4–5

1. RAINBOW.
2. Ice cream.
3. He is wearing his uniform.
4. Corn on the cob.
5. The charcoal in a barbecue.

Pages 6–7

6. The pirates are facing inward, not outward.
7. Rain, hail, or snow.
8. A narwhal (which has a single tusk instead of two, like an elephant).
9.

4	1	3	2
2	3	1	4
1	2	4	3
3	4	2	1

Pages 8–9

10. Bungalow.
11. A somersault: summer + salt.
12. A pencil.
13. A clock.

Pages 10–11

14. Your mother. You are only carrying bags, not groceries.
15. A watermelon.
16. Popcorn.
17. BROWNIES.

***

Pages 12–13

18. They are all girls' names:
    KATY
    RACHEL
    KELLY.
19. Lightning.
20. A mountain.
21. A bridge.
22. A volcano.

***

Pages 14–15

23. There are only three people: Grandfather, father, and son (the grandfather is also father to the father).
24. A potato.
25. SOCCER
    TENNIS
    SWIMMING.

Pages 16-17

26. One crushes boats, and the other brushes coats!

27. The seven seas.

28. None. The boat and the ladder will rise with the tide.

29.

20	(50	50)	15	18
5	16	30	(60	40)
9	(80	20)	30	15
(70	30)	50	10	9
8	40	5	(90	10)

pages 18-19

30. PENGUIN.

31. Stop imagining!

32. A turtle.

33. A starfish.

pages 20-21

34. She asked if he was asleep, and he said, "Yes"!

35. There are twelve "seconds" in a year: January 2nd, February 2nd, and so on ...

36. Say it out loud: Too wise you are, too wise you be, I see you are too wise for me!

37. **NEW YORK**
     LONDON
     BERLIN.

pages 22-23
38. a: 1
     b: 2
     c: 2
     d: 2
     e: 3.
39. Friendship.
40. An arrow.
41. A castle.

pages 24-25
42. Baby giraffes.
43. A mole.
44. a: 3
     b: 2
     c: 3
     d: 3
     e: 2.

pages 26-27
45. CHEETAH.
46. A clock and a sundial. They both tell the time, but the sundial does not work at night.

47. Envelope.

48. A stamp.

49. All of them! And some have even more ...

pages 28–29

50. Yes ... it's highly unlikely that an unboiled egg will crack a concrete floor.

51. Breakfast and dinner.

52. Pea.

53.

2	30	5	15	7
8	4	25	10	3
23	12	11	6	8
4	10	3	27	8
6	21	14	6	9

pages 30–31

54. October.

55. Spinach.

56. Potato (take away "ato" and you're left with "pot").

pages 32–33

57.

2	4	1	3
3	1	2	4
1	3	4	2
4	2	3	1

58. He is bald.

59. A mussel.

pages 34–35

60. Cabbage.

61. Potatoes (pot + 8 Os).

62. Five. You start with 20 oranges each. You'll end up with 15, and your friend will have 25.

63. SWEATER.

pages 36–37

64.

65. The other end of the string isn't tied to anything.

66. Humans. They crawl in early life, walk on two legs as adults, and by the end of their life, they use a walking stick to help them.

67. When it is a chess piece.

pages 38-39

68. A bubble has an inside and an outside.

69. You will always get the answer "four," no matter how many times you attempt it: $2 \times 2 = 4$.

70. The first number was zero, which means it doesn't matter what other numbers are given, the answer will always be zero.

71.

```
3  (19  1) 15  2
(16  4) 8  10  4
11  2 (10 10) 2
4 (15  5) 8  5
10  3  4 (14  6)
```

pages 40-41

72. Neither is right. Two halves of a cake are equal in size.

73. "Language" is the longest word in "the English language."

74. They are all gemstones:
DIAMOND
RUBY
PEARL.

---

pages 42–43

75.

15	15	8	8	10
5	9	10	20	7
7	18	12	5	9
19	4	8	29	1
14	16	8	8	14

76. The whole text does not contain the letter "e," even though it's the most common letter in the English language.

77. "I" is the ninth letter of the alphabet, or "I" is one of the five vowels.

---

pages 44–45

78. PARROT.

79. A snake.

80. Footsteps.

81. Because they taste funny!

---

pages 46–47

82. Just one ... me! When I met them, they were coming from the opposite direction, away from St. Ives.

83. A zebra.

84.

4	2	1	3
1	3	2	4
3	1	4	2
2	4	3	1

pages 48–49

85. NATHAN
SOPHIE
WILLIAM.

86. A ton. Written backward, it spells "not"!

87. Normal. It's usual to have half your fingers on each hand.

88. The letter "d."

pages 50–51

89. Teapot.

90. A hiccup.

91. Water. Cows make milk, but they don't drink it!

92. A bottle.

93. They are all ball games:
GOLF
TENNIS
SQUASH.

pages 52–53

94.

```
1 5 4 4 0 1 3 0 7 6
9 2 5 8 3 8 2 0 4 1
7 3 9 9 4 0 2 5 5 3
2 1 6 3 9 2 7 4 3 0
9 7 5 7 8 0 1 2 0 2
9 2 3 2 6 3 8 6 5 0
0 1 8 9 9 8 0 4 7 0
2 7 4 1 0 6 7 9 2 8
0 0 9 5 2 9 8 5 3 9
1 6 3 4 9 6 3 9 4 5
```

95. Eat, heat, wheat.

96. An egg.

97. A pineapple.

pages 54–55

98.

3	4	2	1
4	1	3	2
2	3	1	4
1	4	2	3

99. The letter "i."

100. Bread.

101. A donut.

pages 56–57

102.   Granny Smith.

103.   Just one to complete it.

104.   A farmer on horseback chewing an ear of corn.

105.   A river.

pages 58–59

106.   The match.

107.   Swallow.

108.   "That's a re-leaf."

109.

20	(50)	(50)	15	18
5	16	30	(60)	(40)
9	(80)	(20)	30	15
(70)	(30)	50	(10)	9
8	40	5	(90)	10

pages 60–61

110.   They are both types of shark.

111.   Yes ... "all that"!

112.   Covering sharks, of course!

113.   Greyhound.

pages 62-23

114.

115.   A brown "e."

116.   Eight carrots.

117.   An apple.

pages 64-65

118.

```
6 4 7 4 1 4 4 2 6 4
8 6 4 5 9 8 8 6 5 2
5 2 6 9 3 2 6 9 4 4
3 8 9 2 7 5 2 8 1 7
4 9 2 3 4 9 5 6 8 5
9 3 5 6 6 3 9 9 0 0
2 5 2 2 0 5 3 0 5 1
0 2 3 1 5 0 7 4 3 8
5 0 8 4 8 1 1 8 6 6
1 0 1 8 9 7 5 9 9 3
```

119.   Snow.

120.   A rainbow.

121.   Daisy is a cow and sleeps in a field.

pages 66-67

122.   Thunderbolt: "th" under "bolt."

123.   An icicle.

124.   The wind.

125.   a: 3

       b: 4

       c: 5

       d: 2

       e: 3.

pages 68–69

126.   SATURN

       NEPTUNE

       MERCURY.

127.   A seashell. If you can hear the sound of the ocean by holding it to your ear, the shell is no longer in the ocean.

128.   Don't worry ... there are plenty more fish in the sea.

129.   The wind.

pages 70–71

130.

131.   TYRANNOSAURUS.

pages 72–73

132. Canoe.

133. The Mississippi River.

134.

8	1	2	2	0	6	9	1	8	6
4	5	4	6	5	4	3	2	9	9
6	5	8	4	4	8	5	9	6	4
9	4	7	3	6	5	7	4	4	2
5	6	3	8	3	2	4	1	8	3
2	9	9	5	5	3	2	3	5	8
1	8	5	1	8	5	1	6	0	3
0	3	0	4	2	1	0	9	2	0
4	0	5	9	1	7	1	5	1	4
1	5	1	8	7	1	8	0	4	9

pages 74–75

135. Chutes and ladders.

136.

L	N	R	S	P
I	J	D	F	G
A	T	M	C	U
O	Y	Z	B	K
X	H	E	V	W

pages 76–77

137.

40	5	15	10	4
5	25	20	12	6
8	15	7	30	15
35	10	10	8	14
11	4	28	17	5

138. They are all insects:

WASP

ANT

BEE.

pages 78-79

139. The fisherman ... if his father's buckets are empty.

140. The ocean.

141. It makes a splash. (Of course it doesn't turn pink! Don't be silly ...)

142.
```
1 8 2 9 6 0 ⓐ 7 1 ④
3 0 ⓵ ⓞ ⓷ ⓼ ⓽ 2 5 4
4 2 5 7 6 0 ⓹ 2 1 ②
0 5 6 1 2 3 9 8 7 9
⑨ 6 4 ⓽ 8 1 7 3 1 3
2 5 7 2 5 7 7 4 6 ⑨
8 3 ④ ⓹ ⓷ ④ ⑦ 3 5 3
⓪ 1 0 ① ⑨ 5 7 ⑤ 4 8
7 3 6 2 6 4 1 6 3 ⑥
2 7 ⑧ 0 1 1 9 6 7 5
```

pages 80-81

143. Lancelot.

144. It was still Mount Everest. Measuring or climbing it didn't change its height.

145. The letter "A."

146. The Mississippi River.

147. Times Square.

pages 82-83

148. GARLIC.

149. Nine. 4 + 5 = 9.

150. Divide.

pages 84–85

151. A skier.

152. Golf. It begins with a tee!

153. He really ought to use a spoon.

154.

3	2	1	4
1	4	3	2
4	1	2	3
2	3	4	1

155. A palm tree.

pages 86–87

156. DOLLAR.

157.

20	20	8	10	6
6	11	9	30	10
5	25	15	10	4
1	22	18	6	11
12	4	32	8	8

158. It has a week-ending.

Pages 88–89

159. They have their backs to each other.

160. Ice.

161. The letter "e."

162.

pages 90–91

163.

```
2 5 6 1 8 2 4 7 3 9
6 6 4 4 2 3 9 2 1 4
3 2 7 2 3 7 5 9 7 1
5 2 9 8 8 0 9 0 6 5
0 5 4 7 7 1 7 6 2 2
8 1 7 9 4 3 4 1 8 9
8 9 5 7 5 1 7 3 6 0
3 5 1 0 2 7 7 2 1 6
7 8 2 9 1 4 1 0 0 2
1 0 3 1 9 0 9 8 9 6
```

164.   a: 4

b: 3

c: 5

d: 1

e: 2.

pages 92–93

165.   A bell.

166.   Silence.

167.   Matt!

168.   They are all colors:

BLUE

GREEN

RED.

pages 94–95
169. a: 3

b: 2

c: 1

d: 4

e: 2.
170. Because they are always spotted.
171. Warthog.

pages 96–97
172. The "c."
173. All four men were married, so no "single" men were there to get wet!
174. A lighthouse.
175. SWEATER

JEANS

DRESS.

pages 98–99
176. ADDER.
177. $888 + 88 + 8 + 8 + 8 = 1,000$
178. Forty.
179. Homework.

pages 100–101
180. Swap the "P" in polar bear, and it becomes "solar bear."
181. A sheep.

182. A snail. (You couldn't carry your home!)

183.

10	25	25	8	11
10	7	40	10	10
30	20	9	14	2
3	12	35	15	4
12	3	42	8	8

pages 102–103

184. Black Beauty.

185. LIMOUSINE.

pages 104–105

186. None. They were babies when they were born.

187. Because he was still alive.

188. The one dated CE 798, since the other must be a fake. No one in the year 368 BCE could have predicted the dating system we use (they wouldn't know how many years BCE it was!).

189.

4	3	2	1
2	1	4	3
3	4	1	2
1	2	3	4

190.

191. Neptune.

192. It's in the middle of water.

193. The smallest possible number is three—girl, boy, boy.

194. 11.

195. The word "wholesome."

196. RASPBERRIES.

197.

198. Bedroom.

199. Fingertips!

pages 112–113

200. They are vegetables:
     LEEKS
     CARROTS
     ONIONS.
201. It's a coin.
202. He should ask one guide, "Which way would the other guide tell me to go?" ... and then take the opposite route. The guide who tells the truth will honestly tell the explorer that the liar will tell him the wrong way. The guide who lies will tell the explorer a fib about the honest man's answer. Either way, the explorer needs to do the opposite of what he is told.

pages 114–115

203. It's a computer lesson, and they are computer mice.
204. A carpet!
205. Your appointment is at tooth-hurty!
206. COFFEE
     LEMONADE
     SMOOTHIE.

pages 116–117

207. a: 3
     b: 9

c: 5

d: 2

e: 4.

208. An octopus.

209. They are so crabby!

210. A river.

pages 118–119

211. They may be lazy or rude, or they may have figured out that there's no way to hide something between pages 57 and 58 of a book, since they are the two sides of the same piece of paper.

212. CE 6. There is no year 0, so when you count, you jump from 1 BCE to CE 1.

213. A mailbox or postbox.

214.

50	5	20	8	11
12	5	40	15	5
6	20	30	25	5
35	20	8	15	15
7	15	5	37	18

(Circled groups: 50 5; 40 15; 30 25; 35 20; 37 18)

pages 120–121

215. JAMES.

216. Sentence.

217. The elfabet.

pages 122–123

218.   Your name.

219.   A needle.

220.   He just went to the hairdresser for a haircut.

221.   CROCODILE.

pages 124–125

222.

223.   A chair.

224.   A nail.

225.   An alarm clock.

pages 126–127

226.   Eyes.

227.   A splinter.

228.   Pants.

229.   They're currencies:
       DOLLAR
       POUND
       EURO.

230.

```
5 6 5 0 6 3 5 1 8 4
6 6 4 6 4 4 0 3 2 8
9 8 7 4 9 7 4 4 6 5
1 1 6 7 1 2 7 8 4 9
2 3 9 8 0 6 1 1 2 3
0 9 2 1 1 3 1 9 1 5
1 8 5 2 0 6 6 0 8 9
4 2 6 4 5 4 8 5 7 1
2 8 1 1 9 8 5 3 3 7
8 3 1 6 4 0 9 6 8 5
```

231.   Saddle.

232.   It's "20 SICK sheep," but your friend will hear "26."

_____

233.   He gets closer and closer, but he never reaches the edge.

234.   A fox.

235.   Out of bounds!

236.   BANANA
        CHERRY
        PEACH.

_____

237.   She got middle-C sickness.

238.   When the two ships meet, they will both be exactly the same distance from the United States.

239.

4	2	3	1
3	1	4	2
2	3	1	4
1	4	2	3

pages 134–135

240. Little Bo Peep.

241. The apple. It is the only one that can be eaten without removing its outer layer.

242. A mushroom.

243. Four minutes. The arithmetic part was just there to confuse you.

pages 136–137

244. The sundae without sauce costs $2.05. The sauce costs 5c, which is $2 less.

245. 10.

246. a: 1
b: 2
c: 2
d: 3
e: 3.

pages 138–139

247.

30	8	20	30	30
10	40	20	9	5
50	10	30	10	8
20	20	6	45	15
42	18	8	20	10

248.   PIZZA.

pages 140–141

249.

4	2	1	3
1	3	4	2
2	4	3	1
3	1	2	4

250.   A chili dog is hotter (spicier) than a hot dog.

251.   A cherry.

252.   There is one "p" in "a pod."

pages 142–143

253.   MILKSHAKE.

254.   California.

255. The truck would have burned off more than 5 grams of fuel by the time it gets to the middle of the bridge. Therefore, the sparrow's weight would have no effect.

256. Ducks or geese.

257. He tractor down!

258.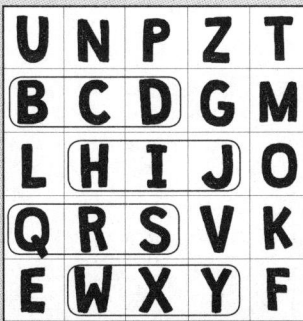

259.
```
5 4 7 9 4 0 7 4 7 1
9 5 5 0 7 1 8 6 5 0
6 3 3 0 6 9 2 8 8 6
6 0 9 3 2 5 4 2 3 9
9 8 6 5 8 3 7 3 4 4
5 2 2 4 5 6 2 1 9 2
3 5 1 8 8 4 1 4 2 1
1 9 5 3 3 2 9 2 5 8
0 3 2 1 4 8 3 5 1 3
4 0 3 6 1 0 8 9 0 6
```

260. The bear has gone in a straight line 3 miles north to the North Pole, then 2 miles onward, now heading south.

261. They don't ... they have bear feet!

262. Because if they lived by the bay, they'd be bagels!

pages 148–149

263.   HELICOPTER.
264.   They are all types of trees:
       BEECH
       OAK
       PINE.

pages 150–151

265.   a: 4
       b: 2
       c: 3
       d: 2
       e: 2.
266.   Seagull.

pages 152–153

267.   A pair of shoes.
268.   A glove.
269.   A turtleneck sweater.
270.   SNOWING
       SUNNY
       RAINING.

pages 154–155

271.   You go on a–head ... We'll follow you on foot!
272.   A shoe.

273. When it's a coat of paint.

274.

3	4	1	2
2	1	4	3
1	2	3	4
4	3	2	1

pages 156–157

275.

2	1	6	3	0	1	3	4	3	3
6	5	9	1	1	8	5	5	9	6
3	8	5	4	8	7	7	8	5	9
5	6	3	5	7	6	9	6	1	7
0	3	4	6	9	5	6	3	4	5
8	4	1	6	3	9	1	4	8	8
8	8	2	4	6	2	0	9	6	1
3	2	5	7	4	0	5	5	2	4
7	0	8	1	2	4	7	1	0	2
1	4	0	2	5	1	2	0	8	3

276.

H	C	E	F	G
W	B	S	X	J
T	U	V	R	D
A	K	L	M	I
Y	Q	N	O	P

pages 158–159

277.

```
1 3 1 0 (6 3 2 0) 5 4
(5 4 6 4 5 7 (4 1 8 5)
 8 9 9 9 7 8) 5 6 (3 6
(9 6 2 8 8 3 8 9 4) 9
 3 (7 8 (6 2 4 6 (8 9) 0
 4 8 2 3 4 1 9 3 (2) 2
(7 1 7 7 6 (9 3 6 0) 4
 1 5 0 5 3) 1 1 7 1 7
 6 4 1 4 8 6 4 5 4 1
(9 3 9 9) 5 2 0 1 8 9
```

278. They are all types of fruit:

APPLE

BANANA

PEAR.

pages 160–161

279. a: 6

b: 3

c: 2

d: 2

e: 1.

280. In a sty-scraper!

281. Cattle.

pages 162–163

282. "Short."

283. A coin.

284. Rosie.

285. FRANCE

SPAIN

ENGLAND.

pages 164–165

286. CHEDDAR.

287. Nacho cheese ("not your cheese")!

288. Lettuce. Just listen as you say it!

289. Edam (read it backward).

pages 166–167

290. True. There are only two capital "F"s. The others are lower case "f"s.

291. None. Acorns grow on oak trees, not chestnut trees.

292. A field of corn.

293.

35	35	20	20	9
15	40	30	10	20
7	19	10	45	25
11	55	15	8	10
6	30	8	60	10

pages 168–169

294. Baguette.

295.

Y	C	D	E	T
G	X	O	P	Q
F	N	L	Z	H
I	J	K	A	S
B	U	V	W	M

296.   The river is frozen.

297.   A horse.

298.

4	2	3	1
1	3	4	2
3	1	2	4
2	4	1	3

299.   When it is a cob (a male swan).

300.   A person riding a horse.

301.   A hippo.

302.   JUPITER.

303.
```
4 5 0 2 9 2 1 1 0 3
2 2 2 4 4 1 9 7 1 5
8 6 4 7 2 8 3 4 5 2
6 8 9 1 5 6 8 8 6 9
9 1 5 4 8 4 6 5 8 8
5 2 8 5 6 9 5 3 3 2
0 4 5 0 3 5 9 9 5 5
1 7 9 6 7 3 0 6 9 4
5 2 6 8 1 7 5 4 2 7
7 7 3 0 2 0 1 8 4 3
```

304.   The noise of the car's engine.

305.   Roller skates.

306. A garbage truck (it is surrounded by flies, the insects, because of the garbage).

pages 176–177
307. You don't; you get down (feathers) from a duck.
308. Lots of animals can. Elephants can't jump!
309. A dog. In the winter, it wears a coat, but in the summer, it wears a coat and pants!
310. They are all types of footwear:
SNEAKER
BOOT
SHOE.

pages 178–179
311. a: 3
b: 1
c: 1
d: 2
e: 4.
312. Garage.
313. Neither; candles burn shorter.

pages 180–181

314. His horse is named Friday.
315. Lioness. Take away "l," "i," "s," and "s," and "one" is left. The lion is "king of the beasts," so she must be queen!
316. "Bye, son!" (Bison ... get it?)
317. BLUE
    YELLOW
    GREEN.

pages 182–183

318. Ruby.
319. Clockwise. It doesn't matter which hand you use, but it does matter whether you're turning the bulb or the socket.
320. A map.
321. Hot sauce.

pages 184–185

322. Persian.
323. They are two sons out of triplets (or more).
324. The more you have, the longer you'll live!
325. A clock.

pages 186–187

326.   A hole.

327.   A deciduous tree.

328.   There are 10. Don't forget the last "g"
       that is part of the question!

329.

40	40	20	15	7
20	5	70	10	20
10	60	20	20	10
10	20	50	30	9
65	15	25	15	10

pages 188–189

330.   They are all types of cats:
       PERSIAN
       MANX
       SIAMESE.

331.

3	2	1	4
1	4	3	2
2	1	4	3
4	3	2	1

pages 190–191

332.

333. None. Peacocks are male and don't lay eggs.

334. Fur or hair.

335. The letter "g."

pages 192–193

336. Glass!

337. The carpet.

338. A key.

339. BLUE WHALE.

pages 194–195

340.

341. Farmer Jennings was walking through town.
342. When it's a greyhound.
343. A veteran.

---

pages 196–197
344. Pickle.
345. They're not into fast food.
346. They're all types of ice cream:
RASPBERRY RIPPLE
TUTTI FRUTTI
CHOC CHIP.

---

pages 198–199
347. a: 3
b: 1
c: 2
d: 2
e: 3.
348. The riddle says it is not to one side of him. That's because it is on the other side of him!
349. A lonfsh.
350. An egg.

pages 200–201

351.

E	V	X	Z	U
G	I	J	K	L
Q	R	S	T	O
M	F	W	Y	N
P	A	B	C	D

352. ROBIN
SPARROW
THRUSH.

pages 202–203

353. HONEY.
354. Teeth.
355. A colander or sieve.
356. A pin and a needle.

pages 204–205

357. PANTHER
LEOPARD
BOBCAT.

358.

8	20	45	45	20
5	80	10	15	9
30	8	10	60	30
50	40	30	15	9
20	10	65	25	20

359. Beehive.

360. First, he takes the rat across and rows back. Then he takes the snake across, but when he rows back, he brings the rat with him. He leaves the rat again and rows over with the grain. He rows back with an empty boat, then finally takes the rat across.

---

361. a: 4

 b: 2

 c: 1

 d: 5

 e: 2.

362. Neither. The yolk is yellow!

363. Seven. He sold four eggs to the first customer (half of 7 is $3\frac{1}{2}$ plus the other half = 4 eggs), and two to the second customer (there are three eggs remaining, and half of 3 is $1\frac{1}{2}$). Add the other half = 2 eggs.) His third customer had one egg. So 4+2+1 = 7.

364. When they are going cheap!

pages 210–211

365. She threw the ball straight up in the air.
366. A tennis ball (and also a volleyball and a shuttlecock).
367. Pawns in a chess game.
368.

3	2	4	1
1	4	3	2
4	1	2	3
2	3	1	4

pages 212–213

369. Two cows in a field.
370. The Moon.
371. One!
372. GREYHOUND
    TERRIER
    POODLE.

pages 214–215

373. Rock and roll.
374.

1	4	3	2
3	2	4	1
2	3	1	4
4	1	2	3

Knock Knock Jokes

This edition published in 2019 by Arcturus Publishing Limited
26/27 Bickels Yard, 151–153 Bermondsey Street,
London SE1 3HA

Written by Lisa Regan
Illustrated by Shutterstock
Designed by Trudi Webb
Edited by Tracey Kelly

CH005154NT
Supplier 40, Date 0719, Print run 9040

Printed in the UK

CONTENTS

CRAZY JOKES 5

HILARIOUS JOKES........37

DIMWIT JOKES 69

LOL JOKES................. 101

RIDICULOUS JOKES.....133

FANTASTIC JOKES 165

SILLY JOKES 197

FOOLISH JOKES 229

KNOCK, KNOCK.
WHO'S THERE?
HUGH.
HUGH WHO?
HUGH DO YOU THINK
YOU ARE?

KNOCK, KNOCK.
WHO'S THERE?
DIDDY.
DIDDY WHO?
DIDDY HURT HIMSELF
PLAYING FOOTBALL?

KNOCK, KNOCK.
WHO'S THERE?
WYNN.
WYNN WHO?
WYNN THE DELIVERY
MAN COMES, SIGN
THE FORM.

9

10

KNOCK, KNOCK.
WHO'S THERE?
LIZ.
LIZ WHO?
LIZ GO OUT TONIGHT!

KNOCK, KNOCK.
WHO'S THERE?
ABBY.
ABBY WHO?
ABBY-CADABRA,
THAT'S MAGIC!

KNOCK, KNOCK.
WHO'S THERE?
METEOR.
METEOR WHO?
METEOR ON THE CORNER IN FIVE MINUTES!

15

KNOCK, KNOCK.
WHO'S THERE?
MUSTAFA.
MUSTAFA WHO?
MUSTAFA SLEEPOVER
SOON, I HAVEN'T SEEN
YOU FOR AGES!

KNOCK, KNOCK.
WHO'S THERE?
SIRIOUS.
SIRIOUS WHO?
SIRIOUSLY, LET ME IN,
IT'S FREEZING OUT
HERE!

KNOCK, KNOCK.
WHO'S THERE?
CONSTANCE.
CONSTANCE WHO?
CONSTANCE SHOUTING
NEXT DOOR IS
GETTING ON MY
NERVES!

19

KNOCK, KNOCK.
WHO'S THERE?
EMMA.
EMMA WHO?
EMMA FRAID I'VE KICKED MY BALL INTO YOUR PLANTS.

KNOCK, KNOCK.
WHO'S THERE?
JEZ.
JEZ WHO?
JEZ LITTLE OLD ME!

KNOCK, KNOCK.
WHO'S THERE?
BART.
BART WHO?
BART TIME YOU FIXED YOUR DOORBELL!

KNOCK, KNOCK.
WHO'S THERE?
FERGIE.
FERGIE WHO?
FERGIEDNESS SAKE, DON'T YOU KNOW IT'S ME?

KNOCK, KNOCK.
WHO'S THERE?
DYNAMITE.
DYNAMITE WHO?
DYNAMITE COME TO OUR PARTY, IS THAT OK?

KNOCK, KNOCK.
WHO'S THERE?
ARNOLD.
ARNOLD WHO?
ARNOLD LADY NEEDS OUR HELP OUTSIDE.

KNOCK, KNOCK.
WHO'S THERE?
JEROME.
JEROME WHO?
JEROME AT LONG LAST, WHERE HAVE YOU BEEN?

KNOCK, KNOCK.
WHO'S THERE?
WAITER.
WAITER WHO?
WAITER MINUTE, MY PHONE IS RINGING!

KNOCK, KNOCK.
WHO'S THERE?
CANDACE.
CANDACE WHO?
CANDACE BE TRUE—YOU PASSED YOUR EXAMS?

29

35

38

KNOCK, KNOCK.
WHO'S THERE?
FARMER.
FARMER WHO?
FARMER DISTANCE YOU LOOK JUST LIKE YOUR DAD!

KNOCK, KNOCK.
WHO'S THERE?
WILLY.
WILLY WHO?
WILLY EVER GET AROUND TO TIDYING HIS ROOM?

KNOCK, KNOCK.
WHO'S THERE?
ESAU.
ESAU WHO?
ESAU AN OLD FRIEND AND HAS GONE AROUND FOR LUNCH.

KNOCK, KNOCK.
WHO'S THERE?
CATH.
CATH WHO?
I KNEW YOU WERE NUTS!

KNOCK, KNOCK.
WHO'S THERE?
LES.
LES WHO?
LES GO AND SEE IF HARRY IS AROUND!

KNOCK, KNOCK.
WHO'S THERE?
ANYA.
ANYA WHO?
ANYA MARKS, GET SET, GO!

KNOCK, KNOCK.
WHO'S THERE?
HOMER.
HOMER WHO?
HOMER GOODNESS! I HAVEN'T SEEN YOU FOR YEARS!

KNOCK, KNOCK.
WHO'S THERE?
COURTNEY.
COURTNEY WHO?
COURTNEY DOOR, I CAN'T GET AWAY!

KNOCK, KNOCK.
WHO'S THERE?
BARBARA.
BARBARA WHO?
BARBARA BLACK SHEEP, HAVE YOU ANY WOOL?

KNOCK, KNOCK.
WHO'S THERE?
YANNIS.
YANNIS WHO?
YANNIS ONE OF THE MOST COMMON NAMES IN THE NETHERLANDS.

KNOCK, KNOCK.
WHO'S THERE?
WENDY.
WENDY WHO?
WENDY WANT ME TO COME AND SEE YOU?

KNOCK, KNOCK.
WHO'S THERE?
ADAM.
ADAM WHO?
ADAMESSY ACCIDENT, CAN I COME IN?

51

53

54

KNOCK, KNOCK.
WHO'S THERE?
ESTHER.
ESTHER WHO?
ESTHER ANYTHING YOU WANT ME TO GET FOR YOU IN TOWN?

KNOCK, KNOCK.
WHO'S THERE?
USHER.
USHER WHO?
USHER BYE BABY, ON THE TREETOP...

KNOCK, KNOCK.
WHO'S THERE?
COLIN.
COLIN WHO?
COLIN A DOCTOR—I'M SICK!

KNOCK, KNOCK.
WHO'S THERE?
FRED.
FRED WHO?
FRED I KICKED MY BALL INTO YOUR FLOWERS, SORRY!

KNOCK, KNOCK.
WHO'S THERE?
SEÑOR.
SEÑOR WHO?
SEÑOR CAR WAS OUTSIDE, SO THOUGHT I'D SAY HI!

KNOCK, KNOCK.
WHO'S THERE?
MISTY.
MISTY WHO?
MISTY MAIL, DID THEY LEAVE A PACKAGE FOR ME?

KNOCK, KNOCK.
WHO'S THERE?
MARY.
MARY WHO?
MARY CHRISTMAS AND A HAPPY NEW YEAR!

KNOCK, KNOCK.
WHO'S THERE?
JESS.
JESS WHO?
JESS WONDERING WHO'S COMING TO YOUR SLEEPOVER?

KNOCK, KNOCK.
WHO'S THERE?
COHEN.
COHEN WHO?
COHEN AWAY, WILL YOU FEED MY CAT PLEASE?

KNOCK, KNOCK.
WHO'S THERE?
DAN.
DAN WHO?
DAN JUST SIT THERE, OPEN THE DOOR!

KNOCK, KNOCK.
WHO'S THERE?
AMIT.
AMIT WHO?
AMIT YOUR SISTER AT THE MOVIES LAST NIGHT!

KNOCK, KNOCK.
WHO'S THERE?
ATLAS.
ATLAS WHO?
ATLAS IT'S SUMMER, NO MORE SCHOOL!

KNOCK, KNOCK.
WHO'S THERE?
JOANNA.
JOANNA WHO?
JOANNA GO FOR A WALK?

KNOCK, KNOCK.
WHO'S THERE?
MICKEY.
MICKEY WHO?
MICKEY IS STUCK IN THE LOCK!

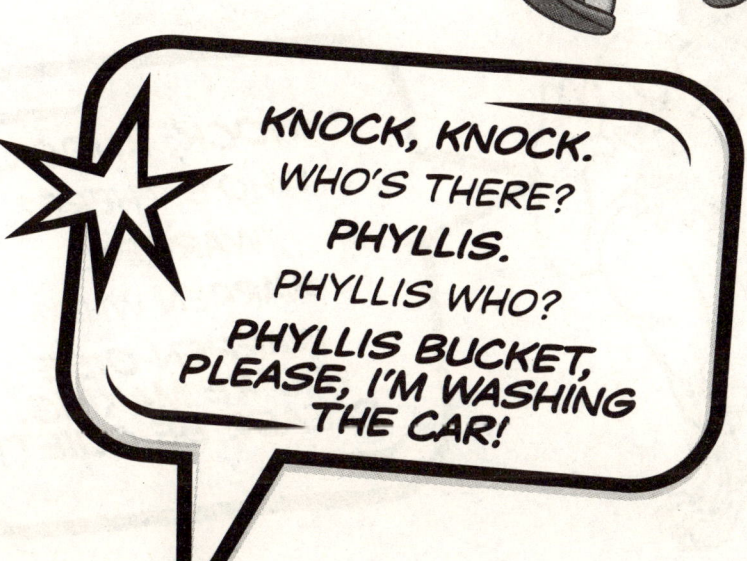

KNOCK, KNOCK.
WHO'S THERE?
PHYLLIS.
PHYLLIS WHO?
PHYLLIS BUCKET, PLEASE, I'M WASHING THE CAR!

70

71

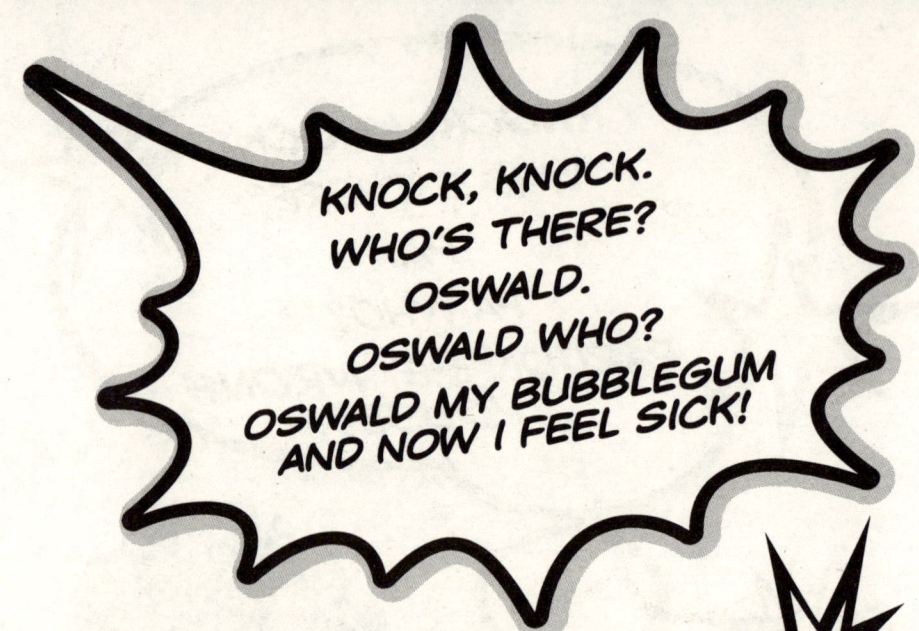

KNOCK, KNOCK.
WHO'S THERE?
ALVIN.
ALVIN WHO?
ALVIN A LOVELY TIME,
COME AND JOIN US!

KNOCK, KNOCK.
WHO'S THERE?
DONUT.
DONUT WHO?
DONUT OPEN UNTIL
IT'S YOUR BIRTHDAY!

KNOCK, KNOCK.
WHO'S THERE?
BOO.
BOO WHO?
AW, DON'T CRY!

74

KNOCK, KNOCK.
WHO'S THERE?
HUGH.
HUGH WHO?
HUGH DID YOU EXPECT
IT TO BE?

KNOCK, KNOCK.
WHO'S THERE?
BAT.
BAT WHO?
BAT YOU CAN'T GUESS
WHAT'S IN MY BAG!

KNOCK, KNOCK.
WHO'S THERE?
DAVID.
DAVID WHO?
DAVID MY KEY AGAIN,
IT'S NOT FUNNY.

KNOCK, KNOCK.
WHO'S THERE?
MISTY.
MISTY WHO?
MISTY DOORBELL AND KNOCKED INSTEAD!

KNOCK, KNOCK.
WHO'S THERE?
ALEX.
ALEX WHO?
ALEX MY ICE CREAM TO KEEP IT FROM MELTING DOWN MY ARM.

KNOCK, KNOCK.
WHO'S THERE?
CAMERON
CAMERON WHO?
CAMEROND 8 O'CLOCK AND WE'LL WALK TOGETHER.

82

84

KNOCK, KNOCK.
WHO'S THERE?
TANK.
TANK WHO?
TANK WHO VERY MUCH!

KNOCK, KNOCK.
WHO'S THERE?
BEAVER E.
BEAVER E. WHO?
BEAVER E. QUIET SO YOU DON'T WAKE THE BABY!

KNOCK, KNOCK.
WHO'S THERE?
PATTY.
PATTY WHO?
PATTY YOUR DOORBELL DOESN'T WORK, I'VE BEEN STANDING HERE FOR AGES.

89

96

KNOCK, KNOCK.
WHO'S THERE?
WANDA.
WANDA WHO?
WANDA IF THERE'S ANYTHING GOOD ON THE TV TONIGHT?

KNOCK, KNOCK.
WHO'S THERE?
VASSAR.
VASSAR WHO?
VASSAR MATTER, ARE YOU CRYING?

KNOCK, KNOCK.
WHO'S THERE?
KENT.
KENT WHO?
KENT YOU DO YOUR HOMEWORK?

99

KNOCK, KNOCK.
WHO'S THERE?
CAESAR.
CAESAR WHO?
SEES HER EVERY MORNING BUT HE'S TOO SHY TO SPEAK.

KNOCK, KNOCK.
WHO'S THERE?
CHRIS.
CHRIS WHO?
CHRIS-PY BACON FOR BREAKFAST, MMMM!

KNOCK, KNOCK.
WHO'S THERE?
FLOUNDER.
FLOUNDER WHO?
FLOUNDER PARCEL ROUND THE BACK FOR YOU.

105

108

KNOCK, KNOCK.
WHO'S THERE?
GIOVANNI.
GIOVANNI WHO?
GIOVANNI GO OUT WITH ME?

KNOCK, KNOCK.
WHO'S THERE?
LETTUCE.
LETTUCE WHO?
LETTUCE IN OR WE'LL HUFF AND PUFF AND BLOW YOUR HOUSE DOWN!

KNOCK, KNOCK.
WHO'S THERE?
JASON.
JASON WHO?
JASON A BALL, THAT'S WHAT OUR DOG LIKES TO DO!

KNOCK, KNOCK.
WHO'S THERE?
BACON.
BACON WHO?
BACON HOT OUT HERE,
I NEED A DRINK!

KNOCK, KNOCK.
WHO'S THERE?
MANDY.
MANDY WHO?
MAN, DE TRAFFIC IS
AWFUL TONIGHT!

KNOCK, KNOCK.
WHO'S THERE?
HEIDI.
HEIDI WHO?
HEIDI-CLARE, THAT
FOOD SMELLS
AMAZING!

114

117

KNOCK, KNOCK.
WHO'S THERE?
LOTTA.
LOTTA WHO?
LOTTA PEOPLE KNOCKING ON YOUR DOOR, AREN'T THERE?!

KNOCK, KNOCK.
WHO'S THERE?
EAMONN.
EAMONN WHO?
EAMONN MY WAY TO THE SKATE PARK, ARE YOU COMING?

KNOCK, KNOCK.
WHO'S THERE?
COLE.
COLE WHO?
COLE ME SOMETIME AND WE'LL GET TOGETHER!

122

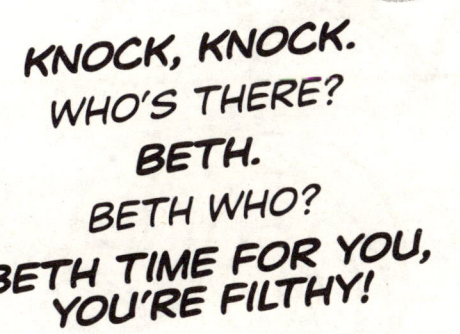

KNOCK, KNOCK.
WHO'S THERE?
HUTCH.
HUTCH WHO?
NOT ANOTHER PERSON COMING DOWN WITH A COLD, SURELY!

KNOCK, KNOCK.
WHO'S THERE?
MARIA.
MARIA WHO?
MARIA ME, I LOVE YOU!

KNOCK, KNOCK.
WHO'S THERE?
KENYA.
KENYA WHO?
KENYA FIX THE DOORBELL SO WE DON'T HAVE TO KNOCK?

127

KNOCK, KNOCK.
WHO'S THERE?
HOUSE.
HOUSE WHO?
HOUSE ABOUT WE HAVE COFFEE AND CATCH UP ON THE GOSSIP?

KNOCK, KNOCK.
WHO'S THERE?
MORRIE.
MORRIE WHO?
MORRIE TRIES TO KISS ME, THE MORE I RUN AWAY!

KNOCK, KNOCK.
WHO'S THERE?
NORMA LEE.
NORMA LEE WHO?
NORMA LEE I'D RING, BUT THE DOORBELL'S BROKEN.

129

KNOCK, KNOCK.
WHO'S THERE?
CATH.
CATH WHO?
OOH, BLESS YOU!

KNOCK, KNOCK.
WHO'S THERE?
MISTER.
MISTER WHO?
MISTER LAST JOKE, DID YOU HEAR IT?

KNOCK, KNOCK.
WHO'S THERE?
ANNIE.
ANNIE WHO?
ANNIE THING WRONG, YOU HAVEN'T BEEN OUT RECENTLY?

KNOCK, KNOCK.
WHO'S THERE?
NOAH.
NOAH WHO?
NOAH GOOD PLACE TO EAT AROUND HERE?

KNOCK, KNOCK.
WHO'S THERE?
ROBIN.
ROBIN WHO?
ROBIN BANKS IS A GOOD WAY TO GET ARRESTED.

KNOCK, KNOCK.
WHO'S THERE?
EWAN.
EWAN WHO?
EWAN-DER IF THERE'S ANY POINT TO ALL THIS, SOMETIMES.

KNOCK, KNOCK.
WHO'S THERE?
FELIX.
FELIX WHO?
FELIX MY FACE ONE MORE TIME, I'LL BE CROSS.

KNOCK, KNOCK.
WHO'S THERE?
OLIVE.
OLIVE WHO?
OLIVE THE TIMES I'VE SEEN YOU, AND YOU STILL DON'T KNOW ME!

KNOCK, KNOCK.
WHO'S THERE?
RON.
RON WHO?
RON HOUSE, SORRY! I MEANT TO KNOCK NEXT DOOR.

KNOCK, KNOCK.
WHO'S THERE?
ALF.
ALF WHO?
ALF OF YOUR ICE CREAM HAS MELTED ON THE DOORSTEP.

KNOCK, KNOCK.
WHO'S THERE?
JOANNA.
JOANNA WHO?
JOANNA PLAY AT THE SKATE PARK?

KNOCK, KNOCK.
WHO'S THERE?
JUANITA.
JUANITA WHO?
JUANITA PIECE OF THIS CAKE THAT I MADE?

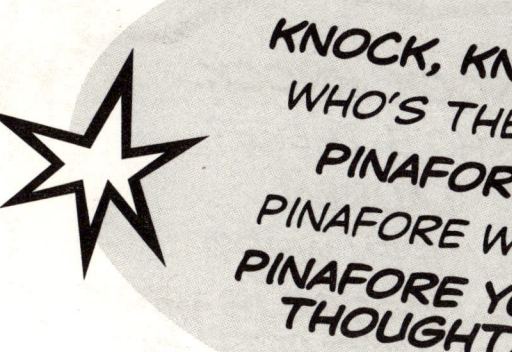

KNOCK, KNOCK.
WHO'S THERE?
PINAFORE.
PINAFORE WHO?
PINAFORE YOUR THOUGHTS!

KNOCK, KNOCK.
WHO'S THERE?
IVAN.
IVAN WHO?
IVAN EARACHE FROM STANDING IN THE COLD FOR SO LONG!

KNOCK, KNOCK.
WHO'S THERE?
TENNIS.
TENNIS WHO?
TENNIS FIVE PLUS FIVE, DON'T YOU KNOW ANYTHING?

154

KNOCK, KNOCK.
WHO'S THERE?
ALBERT.
ALBERT WHO?
ALBERT YOU CAN'T GUESS WHO IT IS?!

KNOCK, KNOCK.
WHO'S THERE?
TURNER.
TURNER WHO?
TURNER ROUND VERY SLOWLY, THERE'S A ZOMBIE BEHIND YOU!

KNOCK, KNOCK.
WHO'S THERE?
SARA.
SARA WHO?
SARA BETTER TIME FOR ME TO COME OVER?

160

KNOCK, KNOCK.
WHO'S THERE?
WAYNE.
WAYNE WHO?
WAYNE-DEER DON'T JUST APPEAR AT CHRISTMAS, YOU KNOW!

KNOCK, KNOCK.
WHO'S THERE?
EMMETT.
EMMETT WHO?
EMMETT YOU HERE BEFORE! DON'T YOU RECOGNIZE ME?

KNOCK, KNOCK.
WHO'S THERE?
DREW.
DREW WHO?
DREW-PY PANTS ARE AN EMBARRASSMENT!

168

KNOCK, KNOCK.
WHO'S THERE?
WILL.
WILL WHO?
WILL POWER IS VITAL WHEN YOU WANT TO LOSE WEIGHT.

KNOCK, KNOCK.
WHO'S THERE?
KHAN.
KHAN WHO?
KHAN YOU COME SKATING WITH ME?

KNOCK, KNOCK.
WHO'S THERE?
CANDY.
CANDY WHO?
CANDY-DATE FOR THE ELECTION, CAN I COUNT ON YOUR VOTE?

KNOCK, KNOCK.
WHO'S THERE?
MABEL.
MABEL WHO?
MABEL HAS BROKEN, AND SO HAS YOURS!

KNOCK, KNOCK.
WHO'S THERE?
SAMMY.
SAMMY WHO?
SAMMY A TEXT SO I KNOW WHEN YOUR PARTY IS.

KNOCK, KNOCK.
WHO'S THERE?
YUL.
YUL WHO?
YUL BE SORRY IF YOU DON'T LET ME IN!

KNOCK, KNOCK.
WHO'S THERE?
TESSA.
TESSA WHO?
TESSA GOOD PERSON TO LAUGH AT THESE JOKES!

KNOCK, KNOCK.
WHO'S THERE?
OWL.
OWL WHO?
OWL TEXT YOU LATER!

KNOCK, KNOCK.
WHO'S THERE?
DELLA.
DELLA WHO?
DELLA-CATE SUBJECT, BUT HAVE YOU BRUSHED YOUR TEETH?

177

KNOCK, KNOCK.
WHO'S THERE?
HARRY.
HARRY WHO?
HARRY UP, WE'RE RUNNING LATE!

KNOCK, KNOCK.
WHO'S THERE?
EDWARD.
EDWARD WHO?
EDWARD DO ANYTHING FOR YOU, HE'S IN LOVE.

KNOCK, KNOCK.
WHO'S THERE?
RAIN.
RAIN WHO?
RAIN-DEER, WITH A SHINY NOSE!

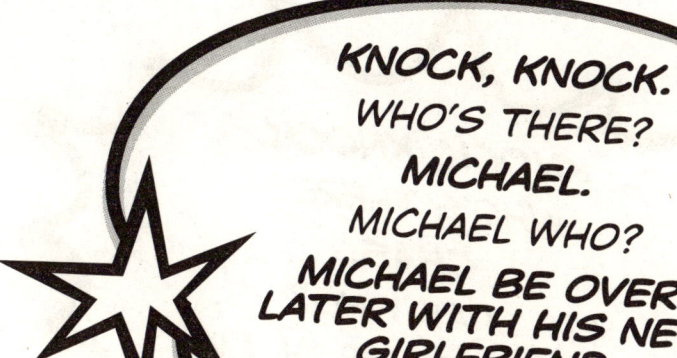

KNOCK, KNOCK.
WHO'S THERE?
MICHAEL.
MICHAEL WHO?
MICHAEL BE OVER LATER WITH HIS NEW GIRLFRIEND.

KNOCK, KNOCK.
WHO'S THERE?
ELIAS.
ELIAS WHO?
ELIAS ALL THE TIME, IT'S HARD TO BELIEVE HIM.

KNOCK, KNOCK.
WHO'S THERE?
IRMA.
IRMA WHO?
IRMA CELEBRITY, GET ME OUTTA HERE!

KNOCK, KNOCK.
WHO'S THERE?
ARTHUR.
ARTHUR WHO?
ARTHUR-NOUR UNTIL WE HAVE TO LEAVE, HURRY UP!

KNOCK, KNOCK.
WHO'S THERE?
CANOE.
CANOE WHO?
CANOE SEE ME THROUGH THE WINDOW?

KNOCK, KNOCK.
WHO'S THERE?
REPEAT.
REPEAT WHO?
OK THEN—WHO WHO!

185

KNOCK, KNOCK.
WHO'S THERE?
RUPERT.
RUPERT WHO?
RUPERT THAT ON THE PATH? I NEARLY FELL OVER IT.

KNOCK, KNOCK.
WHO'S THERE?
FRANK.
FRANK WHO?
FRANK YOU FOR FEEDING MY CAT WHILE I WAS AWAY.

KNOCK, KNOCK.
WHO'S THERE?
MOLLY.
MOLLY WHO?
MOLLY-CULES ARE TOO SMALL TO SEE.

KNOCK, KNOCK.
WHO'S THERE?
STELLA.
STELLA WHO?
STELLA THIS JOKE AND EVERYBODY WILL LAUGH.

KNOCK, KNOCK.
WHO'S THERE?
PAIGE.
PAIGE WHO?
PAIGE YOUR SALARY INTO THE BANK FOR YOU.

KNOCK, KNOCK.
WHO'S THERE?
RICK.
RICK WHO?
RICKETY BRIDGE ON THE WAY HERE, YIKES!

192

KNOCK, KNOCK.
WHO'S THERE?
OTTO.
OTTO WHO?
OTTOLD YOU TO TURN YOUR MUSIC DOWN!

KNOCK, KNOCK.
WHO'S THERE?
THE INTERRUPTING COW.
THE INTERRUPT C—
MOO!

KNOCK, KNOCK.
WHO'S THERE?
SANDY.
SANDY WHO?
SANDY PIZZA MAN TO MY HOUSE!

KNOCK, KNOCK.
WHO'S THERE?
APPLE.
APPLE WHO?
APPLE YOUR HAIR IF YOU DON'T LET ME IN!

KNOCK, KNOCK.
WHO'S THERE?
ANNIE.
ANNIE WHO?
ANNIE TIME GOOD FOR A SLEEPOVER?

KNOCK, KNOCK.
WHO'S THERE?
MAX.
MAX WHO?
MAXIMUM SECURITY ALERT! ALIEN INVASION REPORTED!

196

KNOCK, KNOCK.
WHO'S THERE?
HANNAH.
HANNAH WHO?
HANNAH-LUJAH,
YOU'RE READY ON
TIME!

KNOCK, KNOCK.
WHO'S THERE?
TEX.
TEX WHO?
TEX ONE TO
KNOW ONE!

KNOCK, KNOCK.
WHO'S THERE?
SODA.
SODA WHO?
SODA BUTTON BACK ON
YOUR SHIRT, DUDE!

KNOCK, KNOCK.
WHO'S THERE?
THISTLE.
THISTLE WHO?
THISTLE BE THE FIRST TIME YOU'VE BEEN READY ON TIME!

KNOCK, KNOCK.
WHO'S THERE?
EZRA.
EZRA WHO?
EZRA NO WAY YOU'RE ALLOWED OUT TO PLAY?

KNOCK, KNOCK.
WHO'S THERE?
NOBBY.
NOBBY WHO?
NOBBY AT MY HOUSE SO I WAS LONELY!

205

211

212

KNOCK, KNOCK.
WHO'S THERE?
COSTAS.
COSTAS WHO?
COSTAS A FORTUNE TO GO TO THE RESTAURANT!

KNOCK, KNOCK.
WHO'S THERE?
ASHER.
ASHER WHO?
ASHER NICELY AND SHE'LL MAKE YOU A SANDWICH.

KNOCK, KNOCK.
WHO'S THERE?
ENOCH.
ENOCH WHO?
ENOCH SO MANY TIMES, THEY'VE STOPPED ANSWERING.

KNOCK, KNOCK.
WHO'S THERE?
CHUCK.
CHUCK WHO?
CHUCK THE DOOR AGAIN, IT SHOULD BE OPEN.

225

227

KNOCK, KNOCK.
WHO'S THERE?
SUNDAY.
SUNDAY WHO?
SUNDAY MY PRINCE WILL COME!

KNOCK, KNOCK.
WHO'S THERE?
CARTER.
CARTER WHO?
CARTER TRYING TO SNEAK OUT WHEN SHE WAS GROUNDED!

KNOCK, KNOCK.
WHO'S THERE?
KENNY.
KENNY WHO?
KENNY COME BACK LATER?

232

KNOCK, KNOCK.
WHO'S THERE?
HOLLY.
HOLLY WHO?
HOLLY-LUJAH, YOU ANSWERED AT LAST!

KNOCK, KNOCK.
WHO'S THERE?
DOZEN.
DOZEN WHO?
DOZEN ANYONE LIVE NEXT DOOR?

KNOCK, KNOCK.
WHO'S THERE?
CARMEN.
CARMEN WHO?
CARMEN, LET ME IN!

237

243

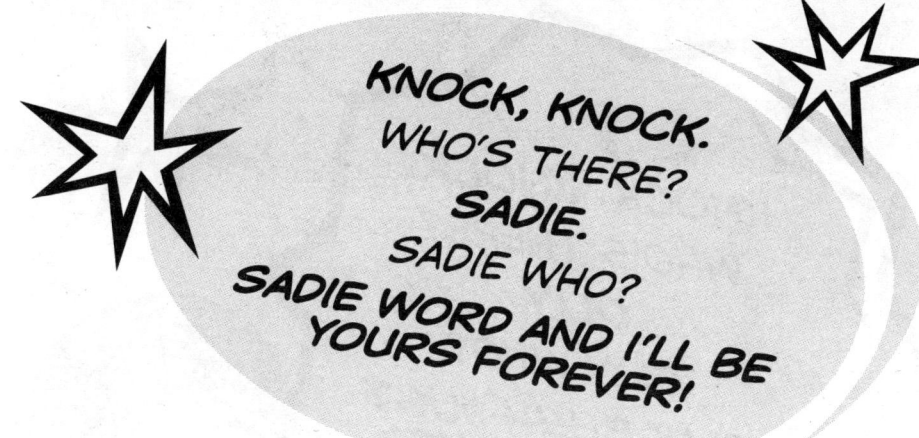

KNOCK, KNOCK.
WHO'S THERE?
SADIE.
SADIE WHO?
SADIE WORD AND I'LL BE YOURS FOREVER!

KNOCK, KNOCK.
WHO'S THERE?
KHAN.
KHAN WHO?
KHAN GO OUT, I'M REALLY SICK.

KNOCK, KNOCK.
WHO'S THERE?
DISHES.
DISHES WHO?
DISHES SUCH A BAD JOKE!

KNOCK, KNOCK.
WHO'S THERE?
CLARA.
CLARA WHO?
CLARA SPACE AND I'LL PUT MY BIKE IN THE GARAGE.

KNOCK, KNOCK.
WHO'S THERE?
ICE CREAM SODA.
ICE CREAM SODA WHO?
ICE CREAM SODA PEOPLE CAN HEAR ME!

KNOCK, KNOCK.
WHO'S THERE?
MISCHA.
MISCHA WHO?
MISCHA MORE AND MORE EACH DAY.

254

255

KNOCK, KNOCK.
WHO'S THERE?
YULE LOG.
YULE LOG WHO?
YULE LOG THE DOOR AFTER I COME IN, WON'T YOU?

KNOCK, KNOCK.
WHO'S THERE?
KIWI.
KIWI WHO?
KIWI STOP TELLING KNOCK KNOCK JOKES NOW?

KNOCK, KNOCK.
WHO'S THERE?
FIVE-EYED ALIEN.
FIVE-EYED ALIEN WHO?
HOW MANY FIVE-EYED ALIENS DO YOU KNOW?!

Just Joking

This edition published in 2019 by Arcturus Publishing Limited
26/27 Bickels Yard, 151–153 Bermondsey Street,
London SE1 3HA

Copyright © Arcturus Holdings Limited

All rights reserved. No part of this publication may be reproduced,
stored in a retrieval system, or transmitted, in any form or by any means,
electronic, mechanical, photocopying, recording or otherwise, without
prior written permission in accordance with the provisions of the
Copyright Act 1956 (as amended). Any person or persons who do any
unauthorised act in relation to this publication may be liable to criminal
prosecution and civil claims for damages.

Written by Lisa Regan
Illustrated by Shutterstock
Designed by Trudi Webb
Edited by Tracey Kelly

CH005153NT
Supplier 40, Date 0719, Print run 9039

Printed in the UK

CONTENTS

1. TERRIBLE TRAVEL 5

2. MIRTH-MAKING MAGIC 47

3. NUTTY NATURE 89

4. FUNNY FAMILY................. 131

5. HILARIOUS HISTORY 173

6. SILLY CELEBRATIONS 215

TERRIBLE TRAVEL

HOW DO LIGHTHOUSE KEEPERS COMMUNICATE WITH EACH OTHER?

WITH SHINE LANGUAGE!

WHAT CAN FLY UNDERWATER?

A WASP IN A SUBMARINE!

WHAT DO YOU USE TO CUT THE OCEAN IN TWO?

A SEASAW!

WHAT IS BIG, FURRY, AND FLIES?

A HOT-AIR BABOON!

WHAT DO THEY SING ON YOUR BIRTHDAY IN ICELAND?

"FREEZE A JOLLY GOOD FELLOW!"

WHEN IS A BOAT LIKE A PILE OF SNOW?

WHEN IT'S ADRIFT!

WHAT FALLS AT THE NORTH POLE BUT NEVER GETS HURT?

SNOW!

WHAT DO YOU CALL A STRANDED POLAR BEAR?

ICE-OLATED!

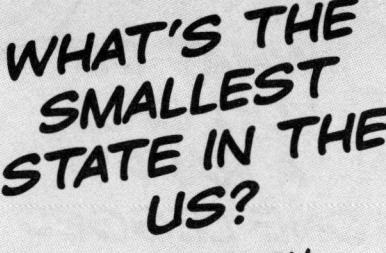

WHAT'S THE SMALLEST STATE IN THE US?

MINI-SOTA!

WHERE DO PIANISTS GO FOR SOME SUNSHINE?

THE FLORIDA KEYS!

WHAT DID TENNESSEE?

THE SAME THING ARKAN-SAW!

WHICH STATE SNEEZES THE MOST?

MASS-ACHOO-SETTS!

WHAT DO YOU CALL A HAPPY ONE-LEGGED PIRATE?

A HOP-TIMIST!

WHY WAS THE PIRATE FEELING SAD?

LONG TIME, NO SEA.

WHAT MUSIC DO PIRATES LISTEN TO?

SOLE MUSIC!

HOW MUCH DO PIRATES PAY TO GET THEIR EARS PIERCED?

A BUCK AN EAR!

WHAT HAPPENS WHEN A PIRATE SHIP GETS OLD?

IT KEELS OVER!

WHY DID THE PIRATE GIVE HIS SHIP A COAT OF PAINT?

BECAUSE ITS TIMBERS WERE SHIVERING!

WHY DID THE PIRATE LEAVE A CHICKEN WITH HIS BURIED TREASURE?

BECAUSE EGGS MARKS THE SPOT!

HOW DO YOU ANNOY A PIRATE?

TAKE AWAY THE P TO MAKE HIM IRATE!

WHERE WOULD YOU VISIT TO SEE A MAN-EATING FISH?

A SEAFOOD RESTAURANT!

WHY DID THE SAILOR CROSS THE ROAD?

TO GET TO THE OTHER TIDE!

HOW DID THE CAPTAIN DO AT SCHOOL?

HE GOT HIGH Cs!

WHAT SORT OF FOOD CAN YOU BUY ON A CHINESE BOAT?

JUNK FOOD!

WHY DON'T ASTRONAUTS GET ALONG WELL WITH MANY PEOPLE?

THEY'RE NOT REALLY DOWN TO EARTH.

HOW DOES AN ASTRONAUT GET HIS BABY TO SLEEP?

ROCKET!

WHY COULDN'T THE ASTRONAUT LAND ON THE MOON?

BECAUSE IT WAS FULL!

WHAT DOES AN ASTRONAUT HAVE IN THE BACK OF THE CAR?

A BOOSTER SEAT!

WHY DO ASTRONAUTS TAKE SANDWICHES ON BOARD THEIR ROCKET?

THEY GET HUNGRY AT LAUNCH TIME!

WHY DON'T ASTRONAUTS HAVE LONG CAREERS?

BECAUSE AFTER THEIR TRAINING, THEY GET FIRED!

WHAT DO ASTRONAUTS DRINK WITH THEIR CAKE?

GRAVI-TEA!

WHAT DOES AN ASTRONAUT DO WHEN HIS TOENAILS ARE TOO LONG?

ECLIPSE THEM!

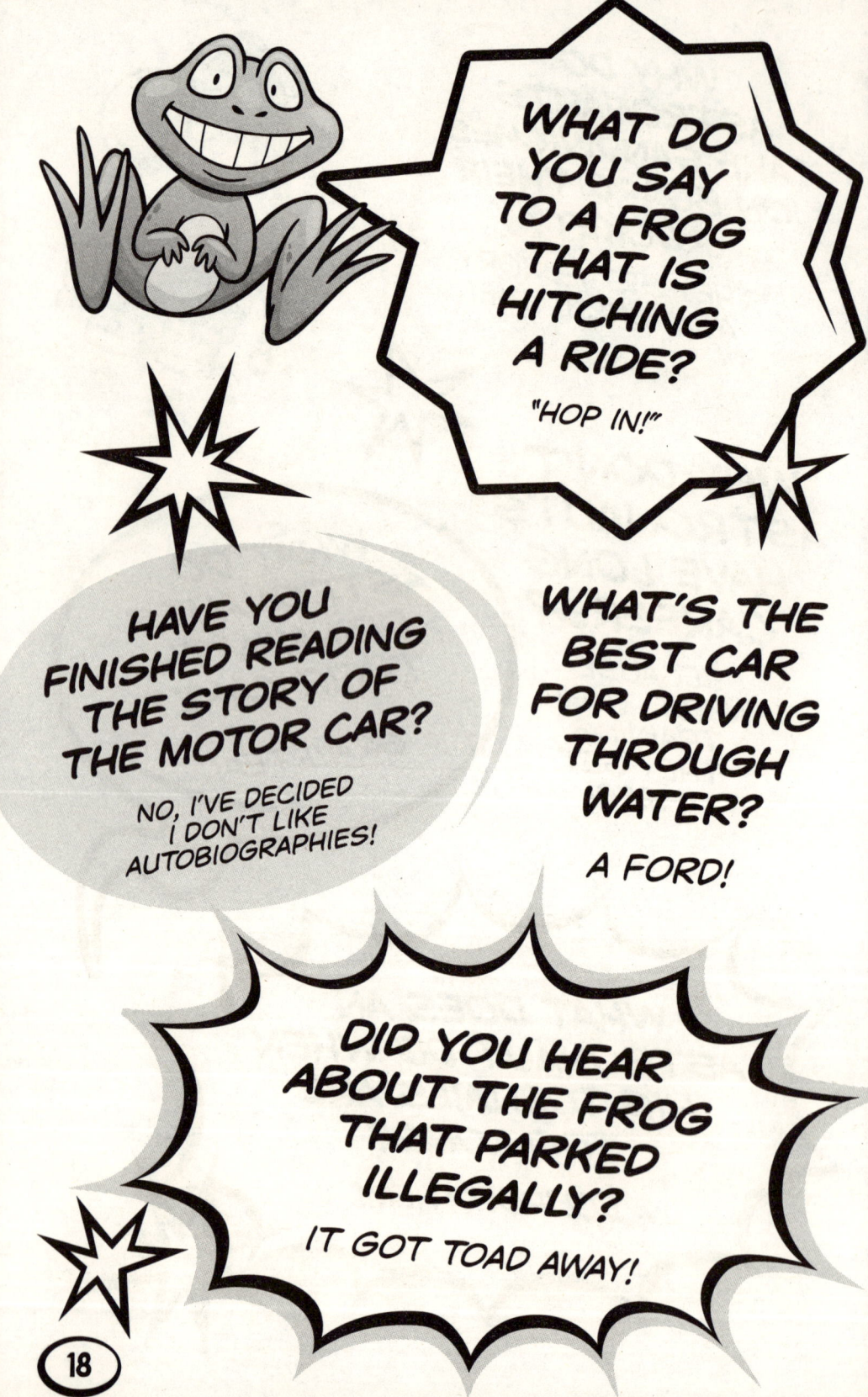

WHAT DO YOU CALL A PIRATE WITH WOODEN ARMS AND LEGS?

BOB!

WHY DID THE PIRATE VISIT THE COMPUTER STORE?

TO BUY AN IPATCH!

WHAT PIZZA TOPPING DO PIRATES LIKE BEST?

ARRRRRRRTICHOKES!

HOW DO YOU GET RID OF A ONE-LEGGED PIRATE?

TELL HIM TO HOP IT!

WHEN'S THE BEST TIME TO BUY A PIRATE SHIP?

WHEN THEY'RE ON SAIL!

HOW DOES A PIRATE TRAVEL WHEN HE'S ON LAND?

BY CARRRRRRR!

WHY CAN'T YOU TAKE A PHOTO OF A PIRATE WITH A WOODEN LEG?

BECAUSE WOODEN LEGS DON'T TAKE PHOTOS!

WHAT DID THE PIRATE SAY WHEN HE TRAPPED HIS WOODEN LEG IN THE FREEZER?

"SHIVER ME TIMBERS!"

WHAT'S THE BEST WAY TO CROSS THE OCEAN?

BY TAXI-CRAB!

WHAT KEEPS ON RUNNING WITHOUT GETTING TIRED?

A RIVER!

WHAT DO YOU GET IF YOU MEET A SHARK IN THE ARCTIC OCEAN?

FROSTBITE!

WHY WOULD YOU TAKE A BASEBALL GLOVE ON A SURFING TRIP?

SO YOU CAN CATCH A WAVE!

WHAT DID THE CRUISE LINER SAY AS IT SAILED INTO PORT?

"WHAT'S UP, DOCK?"

DID YOU HEAR ABOUT THE CUDDLY SEA CAPTAIN?

HE LIKED TO HUG THE SHORE!

WHAT DO YOU NEED TO DRIVE YOUR CAR ALONG THE BEACH?

FOUR-EEL DRIVE!

HOW DO YOU GET TO SEE A SCHOOL OF FISH?

TRAVEL BY OCTOBUS!

WHERE DO PENGUINS GO TO VOTE?

THE SOUTH POLL!

WHAT'S THE BEST THING TO DO ON A TRIP TO THE ARCTIC?

JUST CHILL.

CAN YOU NAME FIVE ANIMALS FOUND AT THE NORTH POLE?

"FOUR SEALS AND A POLAR BEAR?"

WHY DID THE POLAR BEAR CROSS THE ROAD?

TO GO WITH THE FLOE!

WHY SHOULD YOU NEVER ARGUE ON A HOT-AIR BALLOON RIDE?

YOU DON'T WANT TO FALL OUT!

WHERE IS HADRIAN'S WALL?

AROUND HADRIAN'S GARDEN!

WHICH ANIMAL WAS THE FIRST IN SPACE?

THE COW WHO JUMPED OVER THE MOON!

DID YOU HEAR ABOUT THE PIG THAT WENT ON A PLANE?

SWINE FLU!

27

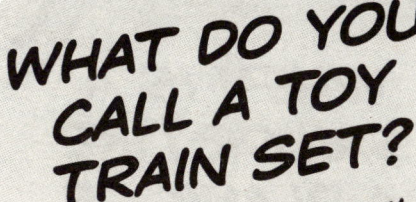

WHAT DO YOU CALL A TOY TRAIN SET?

A PLAY STATION!

WHY DON'T ELEPHANTS TRAVEL BY TRAIN?

THEY DON'T LIKE PUTTING THEIR TRUNKS ON THE LUGGAGE RACK!

WHY DID THE TRAIN DRIVER GET FIRED?

HE WAS TOO EASILY SIDE-TRACKED!

WHERE CAN YOU BUY A TRAIN TERMINUS?

AN END-OF-LINE SALE!

WHEN IS A SAILOR LIKE A PLANK OF WOOD?

WHEN HE'S ABOARD!

WHAT DID THE SAILOR THINK AS HE FELL OVERBOARD?

WATER WAY TO GO!

WHAT KIND OF HAIRSTYLE DO SAILORS HAVE?

A CREW CUT!

WHY WON'T YOU STARVE IF YOU GET SHIPWRECKED BY A BEACH?

YOU CAN EAT ALL THE SAND WHICH IS THERE!

WHY DO SAILORS ALWAYS CARRY SOAP?

IN CASE THEY HAVE TO WASH THEMSELVES ASHORE!

WHAT'S THE BEST DAY FOR SAILING?

WINDS-DAY!

WHERE DOES A SAILOR GO IF HIS SAIL GETS TORN?

TO THE WHOLESALE STORE!

WHAT DO SAILORS LIKE IN THEIR SOUP?

CREW-TONS!

WHY DID THE BRIDGE GET ANGRY?

BECAUSE PEOPLE WERE ALWAYS CROSSING IT!

WHEN IS A CAR NOT A CAR?

WHEN IT TURNS INTO A DRIVEWAY.

WHAT DO YOU GET IF YOU RUN BEHIND A CAR?

EXHAUSTED!

WHY DID THE LITTLE CAR STOP WHEN IT SAW THE MONSTER TRUCK?

IT HAD A NERVOUS BREAKDOWN!

WHAT IS THE HARDEST THING WHEN YOU LEARN TO RIDE A BIKE?

THE GROUND!

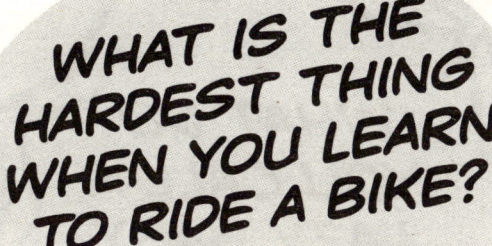

WHAT DID THE BABY BICYCLE CALL ITS FATHER?

POP-CYCLE!

HOW DID THE HAIRDRESSER WIN THE CYCLE RACE?

SHE TOOK A SHORTCUT!

HOW DID THE CYCLIST GET A PUNCTURE?

SHE DIDN'T SEE THE FORK IN THE ROAD!

WHAT DO YOU CALL A LAZY BABY KANGAROO?

A POUCH POTATO!

WHAT DO YOU CALL A BOOMERANG THAT DOESN'T COME BACK?

A STICK!

WHY DO KANGAROOS HATE BAD WEATHER?

BECAUSE THE KIDS HAVE TO PLAY INDOORS!

WHAT ANIMAL CAN JUMP HIGHER THAN SYDNEY OPERA HOUSE?

ALL ANIMALS, BECAUSE THE OPERA HOUSE CAN'T JUMP!

WHAT'S IN THE MIDDLE OF AUSTRALIA?

THE LETTER R!

WHY DID THE EMU CROSS THE ROAD?

TO PROVE IT WASN'T CHICKEN!

WHAT DO YOU GET IF YOU CROSS A KANGAROO AND AN ELEPHANT?

GREAT BIG HOLES ALL OVER AUSTRALIA!

WHAT'S SMALL, FURRY, AND PURPLE?

A KOALA HOLDING ITS BREATH!

WHAT BIRD IS COMMONLY FOUND IN PORTUGAL?

PORTU-GEESE!

WHAT DO INUIT PEOPLE USE TO HOLD THEIR HOUSES TOGETHER?

IGLUE!

WHAT DO YOU CALL A SPANIARD WHO CAN'T FIND HIS CAR?

CARLOS!

WHICH IS THE MOST POLITE TOURIST ATTRACTION IN THE WORLD?

THE LEANING TOWER OF PLEASE-A!

WHY DO THE FRENCH LOVE TO EAT SNAILS?

THEY DON'T LIKE FAST FOOD!

WHAT'S PURPLE AND FISHY AND FOUND OFF THE COAST OF AUSTRALIA?

THE GRAPE BARRIER REEF!

WHICH CAPITAL CITY IS GROWING AT THE FASTEST RATE?

DUBLIN!

DID YOU HEAR ABOUT THE MAN WHO JUMPED OFF A BRIDGE IN PARIS?

HE WAS IN SEINE!

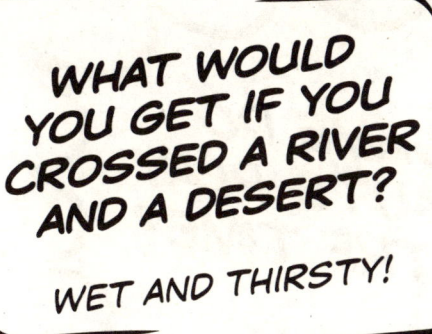

WHAT WOULD YOU GET IF YOU CROSSED A RIVER AND A DESERT?

WET AND THIRSTY!

WHY DID THE SNAKE CROSS THE DESERT?

TO GET TO THE OTHER SSSSSIDE!

WHAT DO YOU CALL A CAMEL WITHOUT A HUMP?

HUMPHREY!

WHY IS IT HARD TO FIND A CAMEL IN THE DESERT?

BECAUSE THEY'RE WELL CAMEL-FLAGED!

WHAT GAME DO ASTRONAUTS PLAY TO KILL THE TIME?

MOON-OPOLY!

WHAT DO ASTRONAUTS WEAR WHEN THEY AREN'T IN THEIR SPACE SUITS?

APOLLO SHIRTS!

WHAT KIND OF MUSIC DO ASTRONAUTS LIKE?

ROCKET AND ROLL!

WHAT INJECTIONS DOES AN ASTRONAUT HAVE BEFORE A TRIP?

BOOSTER SHOTS!

WHY DID THE ASTRONAUT NEED NEW SOCKS?

HERS WERE FULL OF BLACK HOLES!

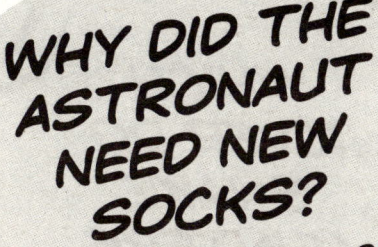

WHAT GOES MOOZ?

A SPACESHIP REVERSING!

WHY DID THE ASTRONAUTS MOVE TO A NEW HOUSE?

THEY WERE SPACED OUT!

HOW MANY PLANETS ARE OUT IN SPACE?

ALL OF THEM!

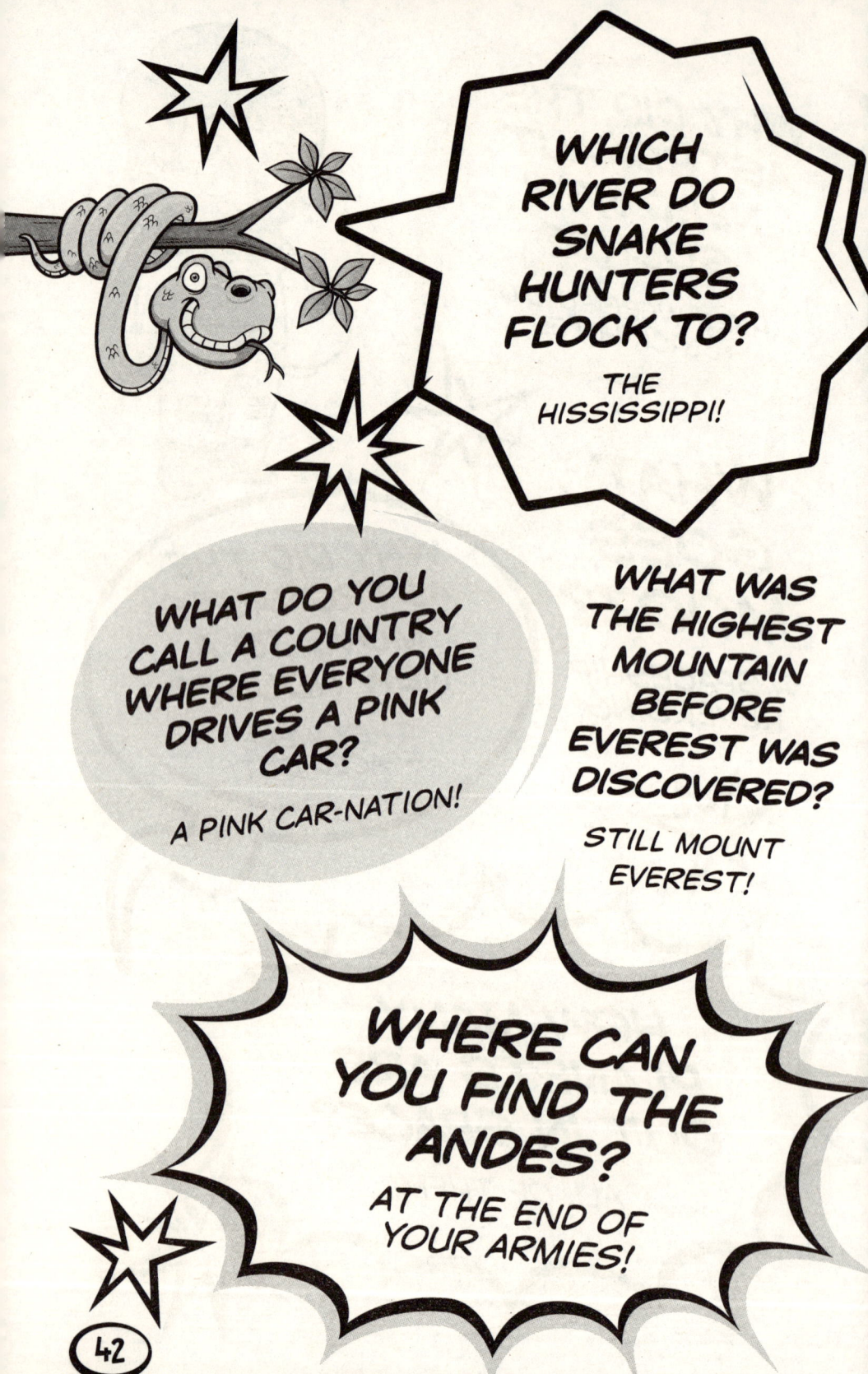

WHY SHOULDN'T YOU BUILD A FIRE IN A KAYAK?

YOU CAN'T HAVE YOUR KAYAK AND HEAT IT!

WHY DID THE BICYCLE STAY IN ITS ROOM?

IT WAS BED-RIDDEN!

WHAT DO YOU CALL A PLANE THAT HAS GONE WRONG?

AN ERROR-PLANE!

WHY CAN'T A BICYCLE STAND UP ON ITS OWN?

BECAUSE IT'S TWO TIRED!

WHY DID THE ROBOT GO AWAY FOR THE SUMMER?

HE NEEDED TO RECHARGE HIS BATTERIES!

WHAT DO SAILORS EAT AS A SNACK?

CHOCOLATE SHIP COOKIES!

WHAT DID THE BREAD DO ON ITS LUNCH BREAK?

JUST LOAFED AROUND!

WHY DO GHOSTS VISIT THE SAME PLACES ON EVERY TRIP?

THEY LIKE THEIR OLD HAUNTS BEST!

WHAT DO YOU CALL A TEDDY BEAR THAT TAKES OFF ITS SHOES AND SOCKS TO PADDLE?

BEAR-FOOT!

WHAT DO YOU CALL A TIGER AT THE BEACH?

SANDY CLAWS!

WHAT ARE MICROWAVES?

THEY'RE WHAT FLEAS SURF ON!

WHAT IS THE BEST DAY TO GO TO THE BEACH?

SUNDAY!

HOW DO TRAINS HEAR?

WITH THEIR ENGINE-EARS!

IF THERE ARE TEN CATS ON A TRAIN AND ONE GETS OFF, HOW MANY ARE LEFT?

NONE, THEY'RE ALL COPYCATS!

WHY DID THE SPY GET ARRESTED AT THE STATION?

HE WAS TRYING TO COVER HIS TRACKS!

DID YOU HEAR ABOUT THE COMMUTER WHO ATE GUM EVERY MORNING?

HE CAUGHT THE CHEW-CHEW TRAIN!

WHAT HAPPENED TO THE FAIRY WHO SKIPPED SCHOOL?

SHE WAS EX-SPELLED!

WHAT DO FAIRIES USE TO TIE BACK THEIR HAIR?

RAINBOWS!

WHAT DO YOU CALL A FAIRY THAT NEVER TAKES A BATH?

STINKERBELL!

WHY SHOULD YOU NEVER SLEEP WITH YOUR HEAD UNDER THE PILLOW?

BECAUSE THE TOOTH FAIRY MIGHT TAKE ALL YOUR TEETH!

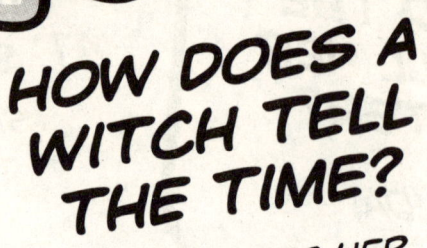

HOW DOES A WITCH TELL THE TIME?

SHE CHECKS HER WITCH-WATCH!

HOW DO LITTLE WITCHES LISTEN TO BEDTIME STORIES?

SPELLBOUND!

WHY DID THE WITCH DATE AN I.T. EXPERT?

SHE WANTED TO MARRY A COMPUTER WIZARD!

WHAT'S THE FIRST THING A WITCH READS IN A MAGAZINE?

HER HORROR-SCOPE!

WHAT DO YOU CALL A NERVOUS WITCH?

A TWITCH!

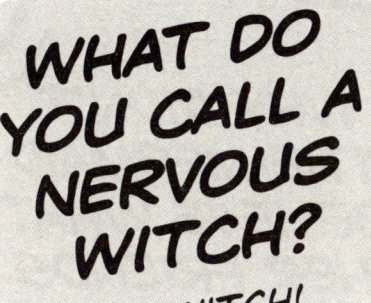

WHY DON'T WITCHES WEAR TOP HATS?

BECAUSE THERE'S NO POINT!

DID YOU HEAR ABOUT THE WITCHES WHO WERE IDENTICAL TWINS?

YOU COULDN'T TELL WHICH WITCH WAS WHICH!

DID YOU HEAR ABOUT THE WITCH WHO SNEEZED AND COUGHED?

IT WAS A COLD SPELL!

WHY DIDN'T THE MERMAID BELIEVE WHAT HER FRIENDS TOLD HER?

IT SOUNDED FISHY!

WHAT DO MERMAIDS READ AT BEDTIME?

FERRY TALES!

WHERE DO MERMAIDS SLEEP?

ON A WATERBED!

WHY DID THE MERMAID BLUSH?

BECAUSE SHE SAW THE BOTTOM OF THE OCEAN!

WHAT KIND OF PHONE DOES A MERMAID USE?

A SHELL PHONE!

WHY DID THE MERMAN HAVE HIS EARS TESTED?

HE THOUGHT HE MIGHT NEED A HERRING AID!

WHY DID THE MERMAN STOP READING A BOOK ABOUT AN ELECTRIC EEL?

IT WAS TOO SHOCKING!

WHAT SPORT DO MERMAIDS AND SEAHORSES PLAY?

WATER POLO!

WHY WAS CINDERELLA NO GOOD AT SPORTS?

BECAUSE HER COACH WAS A PUMPKIN!

WHAT DOES CINDERELLA WEAR UNDERWATER?

GLASS FLIPPERS!

WHY WAS CINDERELLA THROWN OFF THE FOOTBALL TEAM?

BECAUSE SHE KEPT RUNNING AWAY FROM THE BALL!

WHAT'S HUGE, HAS BIG EARS, AND RUNS AWAY FROM A BALL?

CINDER-ELEPHANT!

WHAT DO YOU GET IF YOU PUT A WIZARD AT THE NORTH POLE?

A COLD SPELL!

WHAT DID THE GOLDEN SNITCH SAY WHEN HARRY POTTER WAS BITTEN BY A MOSQUITO?

QUIDDITCHING!

WHAT DO YOU CALL A WIZARD FROM OUTER SPACE?

A FLYING SORCERER!

WHY DID THE WIZARD FLUNK SCHOOL?

HE WAS TERRIBLE AT SPELLING!

WHAT TESTS DO WIZARDS TAKE?

HEXAMINATIONS!

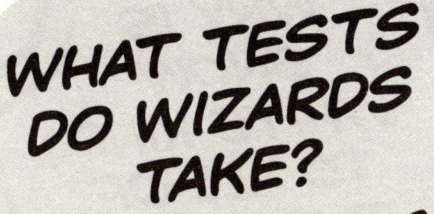

WHY COULDN'T THE WIZARD'S VICTIM MOVE?

HE WAS SPELLBOUND!

WHAT DO YOU CALL A MAGICAL DOG?

A LABRA-CADABRA-DOR!

HOW MANY WIZARDS DOES IT TAKE TO CHANGE A LIGHT BULB?

IT DEPENDS WHAT YOU WANT TO CHANGE IT INTO!

WHAT'S BROWN, FURRY, AND HAS TWELVE LEGS?

THE THREE BEARS!

WHY DID GOLDILOCKS FALL FAST ASLEEP?

SHE WAS IN THE HOUSE WITH THE THREE BORES!

HAVE YOU HEARD THE FAIRY TALE ABOUT THREE HOLES IN THE GROUND?

WELL, WELL, WELL!

WHY SHOULD YOU NEVER TRUST THE BIG BAD WOLF WHEN HE'S IN BED?

BECAUSE HE'S LYING!

WHAT KIND OF MUSIC DO MERMAIDS LIKE?

BUBBLE RAP!

WHY WAS THE MERMAN SO CLEVER?

HE WAS ALWAYS FIN-KING!

WHAT KIND OF HAIR DO MERMAIDS HAVE?

WAVY!

WHAT DO MERMAIDS EAT FOR BREAKFAST?

TOAST AND MERMALADE!

HOW DO YOU GET A MERMAID OUT OF THE OCEAN?

OYSTER UP!

WHY ARE MERMAID'S PARTIES SO POPULAR?

EVERYONE HAS A WHALE OF A TIME!

HOW DO MERMAIDS MAKE A DECISION?

THEY FLIPPER COIN!

WHAT DID THE MERMAID KEEP AS A PET?

A CATFISH!

WHAT HAS A BLUE FACE AND A HORN ON ITS FOREHEAD?

A UNICORN HOLDING ITS BREATH!

WHAT DOES A UNICORN CALL ITS FATHER?

POPCORN!

WHAT'S THE DIFFERENCE BETWEEN A UNICORN AND A CARROT?

ONE IS A FUNNY BEAST, AND THE OTHER IS A BUNNY FEAST!

WHICH UNICORN IS ALWAYS TOP OF THE CLASS?

THE A-CORN!

HOW DID JACK BREAK INTO THE GIANT'S CASTLE?

INTRUDER WINDOW!

WHERE DO YOU FIND A GIANT SCHOLAR?

AROUND THE NECK OF A GIANT'S SHIRT!

WHERE DO YOU FIND GIANT SNAILS?

ON A GIANT'S FINGERS!

WHAT WAS THE NAME OF THE GIANT'S GIRLFRIEND?

FIFI FO-FUM!

HOW DOES PERCY JACKSON CONTACT THE GODS?

HE CALLS THEM ON THE PERSEPHONE!

WHY WON'T YOU GET TO THE UNDERWORLD ON A RAINY DAY?

BECAUSE YOU HAVE TO MAKE HADES WHILE THE SUN SHINES!

HOW DID THE GREEK GOD KNOW WHICH TOOTHBRUSH TO USE?

THE HANDLES SAID, "HIS AND HERMES!"

HOW SHOULD YOU FEEL IF YOU MEET A THREE-HEADED DOG?

TERRIER-FIED!

WHAT DID THE WEREWOLF SAY WHEN IT STUBBED ITS TOE?

AOOOOOOOOWWWWW!

WHAT DAY DO WEREWOLVES LIKE THE BEST?

MOON-DAY!

WHAT'S THE BEST WAY TO GREET A WEREWOLF?

"HOWL DO YOU DO?"

WHAT DO YOU CALL A CREATURE THAT GETS LOST WHEN THERE'S A FULL MOON?

A WHERE-WOLF!

WHY DO WITCHES LOVE HOTELS?

THEY ALWAYS ORDER BROOM SERVICE!

WHY WAS THE WITCH LATE FOR SCHOOL?

BECAUSE SHE OVERSWEPT!

WHAT NOISE DOES A FLYING WITCH MAKE?

"BROOOOOOOOM!"

WHY DO WITCHES GET STIFF JOINTS?

THEY SUFFER FROM BROOMATISM!

DID YOU HEAR ABOUT THE MARRIED MAGICIANS WHO COULD MAKE THEMSELVES INVISIBLE?

THEIR KIDS WERE NOTHING TO LOOK AT EITHER!

DID YOU HEAR ABOUT THE MAGICIAN THAT THREW HIS WATCH UP IN THE AIR?

HE WANTED TO SEE TIME FLY!

DID YOU HEAR ABOUT THE MAGICIAN THAT LOST HIS TEMPER ON STAGE?

HE PULLED HIS HARE OUT!

DID YOU HEAR ABOUT THE MAGICIAN THAT DISAPPEARED DURING HIS ACT?

HE WAS GOING THROUGH A STAGE!

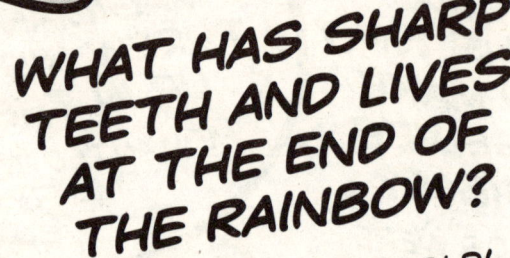

WHAT HAS SHARP TEETH AND LIVES AT THE END OF THE RAINBOW?

THE CROC OF GOLD!

WHY DID LITTLE MISS MUFFET NEED A MAP?

BECAUSE SHE'D LOST HER WHEY!

WHY DID RAPUNZEL GO WILD AT PARTIES?

SHE LIKED TO LET HER HAIR DOWN!

WHO TOLD THE BIG, BAD WOLF HE WAS UGLY AND SMELLY?

LITTLE RUDE RIDING HOOD!

WHERE DO SHEEP GO FOR THEIR HAIRCUT?

BARBER BLACK SHEEP!

DID YOU HEAR ABOUT THE JOKE THEY PLAYED ON HUMPTY DUMPTY?

HE FELL FOR IT!

WHICH NURSERY RHYME CHARACTER TALKS TOO MUCH?

BLAH BLAH BLACK SHEEP!

WHY DOES PETER PAN FLY EVERYWHERE?

HE NEVERLANDS!

HOW LONG SHOULD AN ELF'S LEGS BE?

JUST LONG ENOUGH TO REACH THE GROUND!

HOW MANY ELVES DOES IT TAKE TO CHANGE A LIGHT BULB?

TEN: ONE TO TWIST THE BULB AND NINE TO STAND ON EACH OTHER'S SHOULDERS!

WHAT DO ELVES USE TO SERVE ICE CREAM?

A MICROSCOOP!

WHAT DO ELVES USE TO MAKE THEIR SANDWICHES?

SHORTBREAD!

WHAT SONG DO ELVES SING AT A THEME PARK?

"IT'S A SMALL WORLD!"

WHY DO ALL ELVES LOOK ALIKE?

BECAUSE THERE IS LITTLE DIFFERENCE BETWEEN THEM!

WHAT DO ELVES LEARN WHEN THEY START SCHOOL?

THEIR ELFABET!

WHY DID THE ELF STRUGGLE TO CONCENTRATE AT SCHOOL?

HE HAD A SHORT ATTENTION SPAN!

WHY DOESN'T HARRY POTTER'S GODFATHER LIKE PRACTICAL JOKES?

HE'S TOO SIRIUS!

WHY WAS HARRY POTTER GIVEN DETENTION?

HE WAS CURSING IN CLASS!

HOW DO YOU GET A MYTHICAL CREATURE INTO YOUR HOUSE?

THROUGH THE GRIFFIN-DOOR!

WHERE DO YOU FIND DUMBLEDORE'S ARMY?

UP HIS SLEEVY!

HOW DID HAGRID GET INTO HOGWARTS?

HE USED THE DUMBLE-DOOR!

WHY DOESN'T VOLDEMORT WEAR GLASSES?

NO ONE NOSE!

WHY IS MAD-EYE MOODY SUCH A BAD TEACHER?

HE CAN'T CONTROL HIS PUPILS!

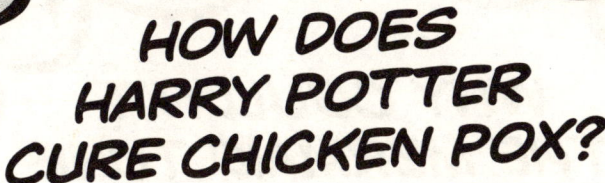

HOW DOES HARRY POTTER CURE CHICKEN POX?

WITH QUIT-ITCH!

WHICH FISH COME OUT AT NIGHT?

STARFISH!

HOW DOES AN OCTOPUS MAKE A MERMAID LAUGH?

WITH TEN-TICKLES!

WHERE DO MERMAIDS WATCH MOVIES?

AT THE DIVE-IN!

WHY COULDN'T THE MERMAID TUNE IN HER RADIO?

SHE WAS ON THE WRONG WAVELENGTH!

HOW DID THE MERMAID TRAVEL TO THE HOSPITAL?

IN A CLAMBULANCE!

HOW DOES A MERMAID WATCH YOUTUBE?

ON THE NET!

WHAT DO YOU CALL A MERMAID THAT SPEAKS FRENCH?

SO-FISH-TICATED!

WHY DID THE OCTOPUS ANNOY THE MERMAID?

HE WAS ALWAYS SQUIDDING AROUND!

DO YOU KNOW THE FAIRY TALE ABOUT THE FROG PRINCE?

REDDIT...

WHY DID GOLDILOCKS STIR THE PORRIDGE REALLY HARD?

BECAUSE DADDY BEAR TOLD HER TO BEAT IT!

WHAT DID HANSEL AND GRETEL SAY WHEN THEY BROKE THE WITCH'S HOUSE?

"THAT'S THE WAY THE COOKIE CRUMBLES!"

WHAT'S WOODEN, HAS A LONG NOSE, AND GOES BOING?

PINOCCHIO ON A BUNGEE JUMP!

DID YOU HEAR THE STORY ABOUT A MISERABLE BEAR?

IT WAS A GRIMM FURRY TALE!

WHAT'S THE TALE ABOUT AN INFECTED TOENAIL?

PUS IN BOOTS!

DID YOU HEAR THE STORY ABOUT THE PRINCESS WHO DRANK TOO MUCH JUICE?

IT'S CALLED THE PRINCESS AND THE PEE!

HAVE YOU HEARD THE STORY ABOUT A POOR LITTLE SPIDER?

IT'S CALLED SPINDERELLA!

WHAT DID THE WITCH DO WHEN HER BROOMSTICK BROKE?

SHE WITCH-HIKED!

WHO IS IN CHARGE OF THE LIGHTING AT HALLOWEEN?

THE LIGHTS WITCH!

WHY DON'T BAD-TEMPERED WITCHES RIDE BROOMSTICKS?

THEY'RE AFRAID OF FLYING OFF THE HANDLE!

WHAT DOES A WITCH BUY AT THE HAIRDRESSER'S?

SCARE SPRAY!

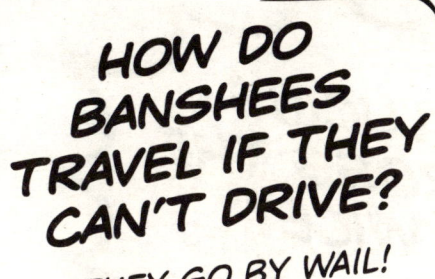

HOW DO BANSHEES TRAVEL IF THEY CAN'T DRIVE?

THEY GO BY WAIL!

WHERE DO AMERICAN BANSHEES GO ON SCHOOL TRIPS?

LAKE EERIE!

WHAT HAPPENED WHEN TWO BANSHEES MET EACH OTHER AT A PARTY?

IT WAS LOVE AT FIRST FRIGHT!

HOW CAN YOU TELL IF A BANSHEE IS POLITE?

SHE ONLY SHRIEKS WHEN SHE'S SPOKEN TO!

WHY DID LUCIUS MALFOY CROSS THE ROAD TWICE?

BECAUSE HE WAS A DOUBLE-CROSSER!

HOW DO DEATH EATERS FRESHEN THEIR BREATH?

WITH DEMENTOS!

WHAT KIND OF BREAKFAST CEREAL DO THEY SERVE AT HOGWARTS?

HUFFLEPUFFS!

WHAT DO YOU CALL QUIDDITCH PLAYERS WHO SHARE A DORM?

BROOM-MATES!

WHAT'S THE DIFFERENCE BETWEEN A STORM AND A HORSE?

ONE RAINS DOWN, THE OTHER IS REINED UP!

WHAT DID THE TORNADO SAY TO THE SPORTS CAR?

"WANT TO GO FOR A SPIN?"

WHAT KIND OF CLOTHES DO BLACK CLOUDS WEAR?

THUNDERWEAR!

WHAT'S THE DIFFERENCE BETWEEN A STORM CLOUD AND A BEAR RAIDING A BEEHIVE?

ONE POURS WITH RAIN AND THE OTHER ROARS WITH PAIN!

91

WHAT DOES A TREE WEAR TO A POOL PARTY?

SWIMMING TRUNKS!

HOW DO YOU DESCRIBE AN ACORN?

IN A NUTSHELL, IT'S AN OAK TREE!

WHAT KIND OF CAR DOES A FARMER DRIVE?

A CORN-VERTIBLE!

WHAT DID THE TREE DO WHEN THE LIBRARY WAS CLOSED?

IT TRIED ANOTHER BRANCH!

WHAT TWO FISH DO SHOE-REPAIRERS LIKE BEST?

SOLES AND EELS!

WHAT GAME CAN YOU PLAY AT THE SEASIDE?

TIDE AND SEEK!

WHAT LIES AT THE BOTTOM OF THE OCEAN AND WON'T MOVE?

A NERVOUS WRECK!

WHY DON'T WHALES WATCH SAD MOVIES?

IT MAKES THEM BLUBBER!

WHAT DID THE CRAB SAY TO HER GROUCHY HUSBAND?

"DON'T GET SNAPPY WITH ME!"

WHAT DO YOU CALL A BABY CRAB?

A LITTLE NIPPER!

WHY DO WHALES SING?

BECAUSE THEY CAN'T TALK!

WHY DON'T DOLPHINS PLAY POKER FOR MONEY?

BECAUSE OF ALL THE CARD SHARKS!

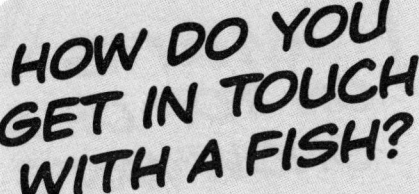

HOW DO YOU GET IN TOUCH WITH A FISH?

YOU DROP IT A LINE!

HOW DOES A FISH SAVE ITS MONEY?

IT GOES TO THE RIVERBANK!

WHY ARE FISH SO CLEVER?

THEY SWIM IN SCHOOLS!

WHY WASN'T THE OCTOPUS AFRAID OF BEING ATTACKED?

IT WAS WELL ARMED!

WHAT DID THE FOUR-BY-FOUR OWNER SAY IN THE BLIZZARD?

"SNOW PROBLEM!"

HOW FAST DOES LIGHT TRAVEL?

I DON'T KNOW, BUT IT GETS HERE WAY TOO EARLY IN THE MORNING!

HOW DO YOU GET ICE OFF A HOT-AIR BALLOON?

USE A SKYSCRAPER!

WHAT DOES THE SUN DRINK OUT OF?

SUNGLASSES!

WHY DID THE
VULTURES ARGUE?

THEY HAD A BONE TO
PICK WITH EACH OTHER!

WHERE DO
TADPOLES
CHANGE INTO
FROGS?

IN THE
CROAKROOM!

WHAT DO YOU
CALL A MAN
WHO LIVES WILD
WITH A PACK OF
WOLVES?

WOLFGANG!

WHAT LIVES IN
THE FOREST
AND REPEATS
ITSELF?

A WILD BOAR.

WHAT KIND OF ANIMAL WILL NEVER OVERSLEEP?

A LLAMA CLOCK!

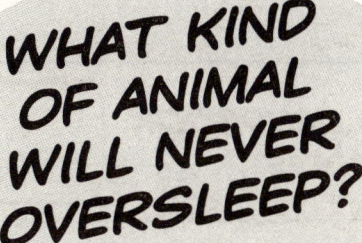

WHY IS IT HARD TO SPOT A CAMEL?

THEY ARE WELL CAMEL-FLAGED!

WHAT DO HORSES WEAR AT THE BEACH?

CLIP-CLOPS!

WHAT KIND OF ANIMAL IS BEST AT BREAK DANCING?

A HIP-HOP-POTAMUS!

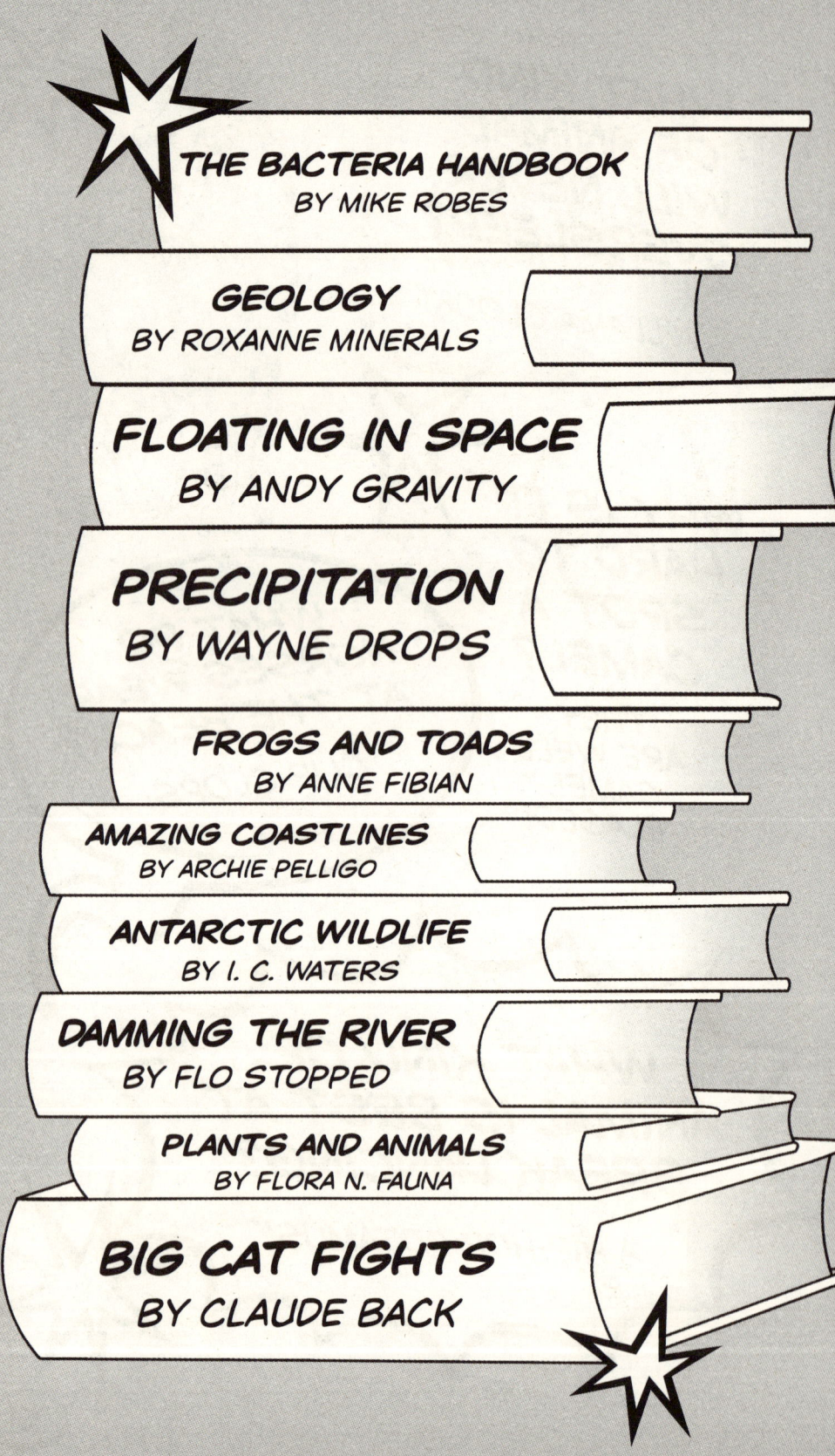

WHAT SHOULD YOU DO IN THE PRESENCE OF A MIGHTY TREE?

TAKE A BOUGH!

WHAT DO YOU CALL A WASP?

A WANNA-BEE!

DID YOU HEAR ABOUT THE BEE BORN IN THE SPRING?

IT WAS A MAY-BEE!

WHY IS THE LETTER A LIKE A FLOWER?

BECAUSE A B COMES AFTER IT!

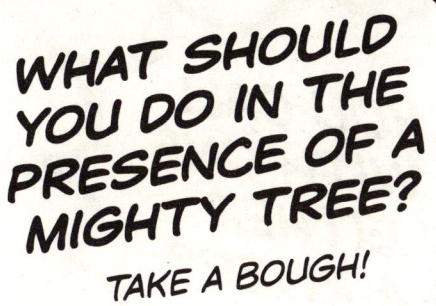

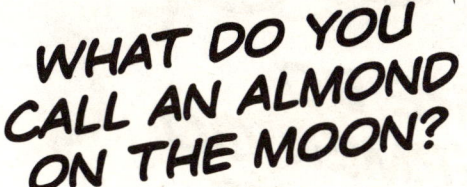

WHAT DO YOU CALL AN ALMOND ON THE MOON?

AN ASTRO-NUT!

HOW DO OBJECTS STAY IN ORBIT? BECAUSE THEY'RE SATEL-LIGHT!

WHAT'S BIG, BRIGHT, AND STUPID?

A FOOL MOON!

DID YOU HEAR THE JOKE ABOUT THE MOON? IT WAS OUT OF THIS WORLD!

WHERE DO WEATHERMEN GO FOR A DRINK?

THE CLOSEST ISOBAR!

WHAT DID ONE HURRICANE SAY TO THE OTHER?

"I HAVE MY EYE ON YOU!"

WHAT DO YOU SAY WHEN IT RAINS DUCKS AND CHICKENS?

"FOWL WEATHER, ISN'T IT?"

WHAT DID ONE TORNADO SAY TO THE OTHER?

"LET'S TWIST AGAIN LIKE WE DID LAST SUMMER!"

WHAT DID ONE RAINDROP SAY TO THE OTHER?

"TWO'S COMPANY, THREE'S A CLOUD!"

WHAT WAS THE WORST KIND OF WEATHER IN CAESAR'S DAYS?

ALL HAIL!

WHAT'S WORSE THAN RAINING CATS AND DOGS?

HAILING TAXIS!

DID YOU HEAR ABOUT THE HAPPY RAINDROP?

IT WAS ON CLOUD 9!

WHAT MONTH DO LUMBERJACKS LIKE THE BEST?

SEP-TIMBER!

WHY DO TREES HATE EXAMS?

THEY ARE EASILY STUMPED!

WHAT DID THE BEAVER SAY TO THE TREE?

"IT'S BEEN NICE GNAWING YOU!"

WHAT DID THE TREE SAY TO THE WOODPECKER?

"LEAF ME ALONE!"

WHAT'S THE DIFFERENCE BETWEEN AN OAK TREE AND A TIGHT SHOE?

ONE MAKES ACORNS, THE OTHER MAKES CORNS ACHE!

WHAT KIND OF TREES DO MATHEMATICIANS LIKE?

GEOMETREES AND TRIGONOMETREES!

WHAT DID ONE FLOWER SAY TO THE OTHER?

"WHAT'S UP, BUD?"

WHY DIDN'T ANYONE LAUGH AT THE FARMER'S JOKES?

THEY WERE TOO CORNY!

WHY IS IT HARD TO WIND UP A SNAKE?

YOU CAN'T PULL ITS LEG!

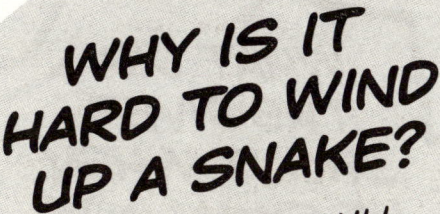

WHY DIDN'T THE VIPER VIPER NOSE?

BECAUSE THE ADDER ADDER HANDKERCHIEF!

WHY COULDN'T THE SNAKE SAY ANYTHING?

IT HAD A FROG IN ITS THROAT!

DID YOU HEAR ABOUT THE SNAKE THAT WAS TRYING TO IMPRESS ITS DATE?

IT WAS A SNAKE CHARMER!

WHAT DID THE DIVER SHOUT WHEN HE SWAM INTO A SEAWEED FOREST?

"KELP!"

DO FISH LIKE TO WATCH BASEBALL?

YES–THERE ARE 20,000 LEAGUES UNDER THE SEA!

WHAT ARE LITTLE SEA CREATURES MOST AFRAID OF?

SQUID-NAPPERS!

WHY DO FISH IN A SCHOOL ALL SWIM IN THE SAME DIRECTION?

THEY'RE PLAYING SALMON SAYS!

WHAT IS IN THE MIDDLE OF A JELLYFISH?

ITS JELLYBUTTON!

WHAT SEA CREATURE WANTS TO BE LEFT ALONE?

A HERMIT CRAB!

WHAT IS THE SADDEST CREATURE IN THE OCEAN?

THE BLUE WHALE!

WHY DID THE SHARK BANG ITS HEAD AGAINST THE BOTTOM OF THE SHIP?

IT WAS A HAMMERHEAD!

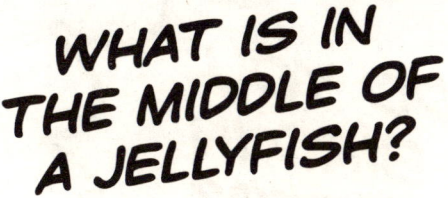

WHAT DO YOU CALL A BIRD IN THE WINTER?

A BRRRRR-D!

HOW DO YOU CATCH A UNIQUE BIRD?

UNIQUE UP ON IT!

HOW DO YOU CATCH A TAME BIRD?

THE TAME WAY, UNIQUE UP ON IT!

WHAT DID THE BIRD SAY AS IT FINISHED BUILDING ITS NEST?

"THAT'S THE LAST STRAW!"

WHY ARE FROGS ALWAYS HAPPY?

BECAUSE THEY CAN EAT WHATEVER BUGS THEM!

WHAT DID THE COW SAY WHEN IT WAS HUNGRY?

"THISTLE HAVE TO DO!"

WHAT DID THE SPIDER SAY WHEN ITS WEB GOT BROKEN?

"DARN IT!"

WHY DO MALE DEER NEED BRACES?

BECAUSE THEY HAVE BUCK TEETH!

CINDY: DID YOU KNOW IT'S RAINING CATS AND DOGS OUT THERE?

MINDY: I KNOW, I JUST STEPPED IN A POODLE!

WHAT'S THE DIFFERENCE BETWEEN WEATHER AND CLIMATE?

YOU CAN'T WEATHER A TREE, BUT YOU CAN CLIMATE!

WHY SHOULDN'T YOU ARGUE WITH A WEATHERMAN?

HE MIGHT STORM OUT ON YOU!

WHY DID THE MAN TAKE HIS WALLET OUT INTO THE STORM?

HE WAS HOPING FOR SOME CHANGE IN THE WEATHER!

WHAT DID THE WEATHER WOMAN USE TO CURL HER HAIR?

A HEAT WAVE!

WHY DID THE THERMOMETER GO TO COLLEGE?

TO GET A DEGREE!

DENNY: MY STUPID BROTHER TRIED TO CATCH FOG YESTERDAY.

LENNY: DON'T TELL ME – HE MIST?

DID YOU HEAR THAT DOROTHY AND TOTO GOT CAUGHT IN A STORM?

IT WAS THE BLIZZARD OF OZ!

WHY DID HUMPTY DUMPTY HAVE A GREAT FALL?

TO MAKE UP FOR A MISERABLE SUMMER!

WHAT DID THE BOY SAY AFTER READING FOR TOO LONG IN THE SUN?

"HMM, I'M CERTAINLY WELL RED!"

MAISIE: TEACHER SAYS WE'RE DOING OUR TEST TODAY, COME RAIN OR SHINE.

DAISY: YAY! IT'S SNOWING!

WHAT KIND OF WEATHER IS GOOD WHEN YOU'RE DINING OUT?

FORK LIGHTNING!

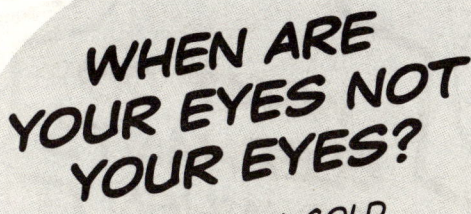

WHEN ARE YOUR EYES NOT YOUR EYES?

WHEN A COLD WIND MAKES THEM WATER!

WHEN DO MONKEYS FALL FROM THE SKY?

DURING APE-RIL SHOWERS!

WHAT DID THE KNITTED HAT SAY TO THE SCARF?

"YOU HANG AROUND WHILE I GO ON AHEAD!"

WHAT DID THE TREE SAY AFTER WINTER HAD PASSED?

WHAT A RE-LEAF!

WHAT DO OAKS LEARN AT SCHOOL?

THEIR TREE TIMES TABLE!

HOW HARD IS IT TO COUNT SYCAMORES?

IT'S AS EASY AS ONE, TWO, TREE!

WHAT DID THE LEAF SAY WHEN IT FELL FROM THE TREE?

NOTHING, LEAVES DON'T TALK!

WHY AREN'T TREES GOOD AT QUIZZES?

BECAUSE THEY'RE OFTEN STUMPED!

HOW DO YOU GET RID OF AN ANNOYING WASP?

TELL IT TO BUZZ OFF!

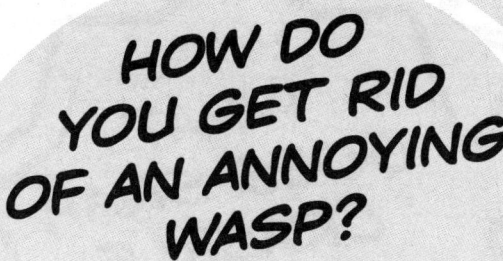

WHAT GIFT DID THE SMELLY BEE RECEIVE FROM ITS FRIENDS?

BEE-ODORANT!

WHAT DO YOU CALL A BEE THAT IS UNHAPPY?

A GRUMBLEBEE!

DID YOU HEAR ABOUT THE BEE THAT SMELLED BAD?

IT HAD BEE-O!

WHAT GOES SNAP, CRACKLE, POP?

A FIREFLY WITH A SHORT CIRCUIT!

WHAT'S THE LARGEST MOTH IN THE WORLD?

A MAMMOTH!

WHAT DID THE WORM SAY TO HER SON WHEN HE CAME HOME LATE?

"WHERE IN EARTH HAVE YOU BEEN?"

WHAT DO YOU CALL A FLY WITH NO WINGS?

A WALK!

WHERE DO BEES GO WHEN THEY NEED TO USE THE BATHROOM?

THE BP STATION!

WHAT DO YOU CALL AN INTERFERING BEE?

A BUZZYBODY!

HOW CAN YOU TELL A WORM'S HEAD FROM ITS TAIL?

TICKLE THE MIDDLE, AND SEE WHICH END LAUGHS!

WHAT DID THE BEE SHOUT WHEN THE HIVE WAS UNDER ATTACK?

"BEE-WARE!"

FUNNY FAMILY

WHY WAS THE YOUNGEST OF SEVEN CHILDREN LATE FOR SCHOOL?

BECAUSE THE ALARM WAS SET FOR SIX!

TEACHER: WHAT IS THE PLURAL OF BABY?

FRANCES: TWINS!

TEACHER: DID YOUR MOTHER HELP YOU WITH YOUR HOMEWORK?

CHARLIE: NO, I GOT IT WRONG ALL BY MYSELF!

DAD: WHY DIDN'T YOU COME STRAIGHT HOME FROM SCHOOL?

SEBASTIAN: BECAUSE WE LIVE AROUND THE CORNER!

WHY DID DAD TAKE HIS RAZOR TO SPORTS DAY?

HE WANTED TO SHAVE A FEW SECONDS OFF HIS TIME!

EMILY: DAD, I GOT AN A IN SPELLING!

DAD: YOU FOOL, THERE ISN'T AN A IN SPELLING!

GRANDMA: I HEAR YOU'VE BEEN MISSING SCHOOL?

BRADLEY: THAT'S A LIE. I HAVEN'T MISSED IT ONE BIT!

DID YOU HEAR ABOUT THE EMBARRASSING TWINS IN THE LONG DISTANCE RACE?

ONE RAN IN SHORT BURSTS, THE OTHER RAN IN BURST SHORTS!

TILLY: MY AUNT HAS ONE LEG LONGER THAN THE OTHER.

BILLY: IS SHE CALLED EILEEN?

DAD, I CAN'T MOW THE LAWN TODAY, I'VE TWISTED MY ANKLE.

THAT'S A LAME EXCUSE!

WHY DID GRANDPA PUT WHEELS ON HIS ROCKING CHAIR?

HE WANTED TO ROCK AND ROLL!

DAD, I KEEP THINKING I'M A WOODWORM!

WELL, SON, LIFE DOES GET BORING SOMETIMES!

WHAT DO YOU GET IF YOU CROSS DAD'S SOCKS WITH A BOOMERANG?

A NASTY SMELL THAT KEEPS COMING BACK!

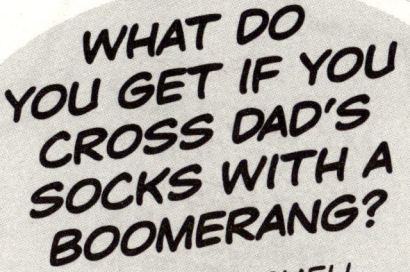

ANNIE: YOUR AUNT LOOKS SO OLD!

DANNY: YES, SHE'S AN AUNT-IQUE!

KATE: OUR MOTHER IS EXCELLENT AT HISTORY BUT AN AWFUL COOK.

NATE: I KNOW, SHE'S AN EXPERT ON ANCIENT GREASE!

WHY DOES YOUR SISTER PUT GLUE ON HER SALAD?

SHE WANTS TO STICK TO HER DIET!

MY BROTHER IS SO DUMB, HE FOUND THREE MILK CARTONS IN A FIELD AND THOUGHT IT WAS A COW'S NEST!

MY BROTHER IS SO DUMB, HE DRINKS HOT CHOCOLATE AT NIGHT SO HE WILL HAVE SWEET DREAMS!

MY BROTHER IS SO DUMB, HE THINKS GLUTEUS MAXIMUS IS A ROMAN EMPEROR!

MY BROTHER IS SO DUMB, HE WENT LOOKING FOR A HILLY LAKE SO HE COULD WATER SKI!

WHAT ANCIENT GREEK LAND IS LIKE YOUR BROTHER'S BEDROOM?

MESS-OPOTAMIA!

WHAT CLOTHES DOES A HOUSE WEAR?

ADDRESS!

WHAT DID THE ITALIAN SAY WHEN HE RETURNED FROM AN OVERSEAS TRIP?

"ROME, SWEET ROME!"

HOW MANY KIDS DOES IT TAKE TO CHANGE A LIGHT BULB?

THREE—ONE TO SAY, "BUT I DIDN'T LEAVE IT ON," AND TWO TO SAY, "BUT I CHANGED IT LAST TIME!"

WINNIE: WHY IS THERE A PLANE OUTSIDE YOUR BEDROOM DOOR?

VINNIE: I MUST HAVE LEFT THE LANDING LIGHT ON!

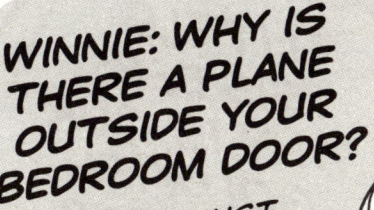

WHAT KIND OF MONSTER LIVES IN YOUR BROTHER'S ROOM?

THE LOCH MESS MONSTER!

JAN: HOW CAN YOU FIT TWENTY FRIENDS IN YOUR ROOM AT ONCE AND STILL PLAY A GAME?

STAN: WE'RE PLAYING SQUASH!

DAD: THERE'S A BURGLAR DOWNSTAIRS EATING THE CAKE YOUR SISTER BAKED.

HUGH: SHOULD I CALL THE POLICE OR AN AMBULANCE?

LITTLE SISTER: WHY IS OUR GOLDFISH ORANGE?

BIG BROTHER: BECAUSE THE WATER MAKES IT RUSTY!

DID YOU HEAR ABOUT THE GUPPY THAT WENT TO HOLLYWOOD?

IT BECAME A STARFISH!

KIM: WHY IS YOUR DRAWING OF A FISH SO TINY?

TIM: I'VE DRAWN IT TO SCALE!

WHAT IS STRANGER THAN SEEING A CAT FISH?

SEEING A GOLDFISH BOWL!

WHEN DOES A PET CAT GO "MOO?"

WHEN IT IS LEARNING A NEW LANGUAGE!

WHERE CAN YOU TAKE A PET CAT FOR A DAY TRIP?

TO THE MEW-SEUM!

WHAT DID THE CAT SAY TO THE FLEA?

"STOP BUGGING ME!"

WHAT IS IT CALLED WHEN YOUR PET CAT WINS A DOG SHOW?

A CAT-ASTROPHE!

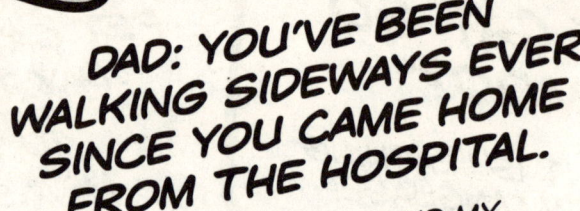

DAD: YOU'VE BEEN WALKING SIDEWAYS EVER SINCE YOU CAME HOME FROM THE HOSPITAL.

HANNAH: THEY SAID MY MEDICINE MIGHT HAVE SIDE EFFECTS...

BOBBY: WHAT'S THE DIFFERENCE BETWEEN A HILL AND A PILL?

ROBBIE: A HILL IS HARD TO GET UP, BUT A PILL IS HARD TO GET DOWN.

WHAT DID THE MOTHER BROOM SAY TO HER SON?

IT'S TIME TO GO TO SWEEP!

WHAT CAN YOU GIVE AND KEEP AT THE SAME TIME?

A COLD!

CARRIE: HOW DID DAD GET AN INJURY ON A FISHING TRIP?

HARRY: HE PULLED A MUSSEL!

WHY DID THE HOUSE GO TO THE EMERGENCY ROOM?

BECAUSE IT HAD A WINDOW PANE!

MOTHER: YOU SHOULDN'T PLAY BALL TODAY, SON, YOU HAVE A SICKNESS BUG.

JIM: I KNOW, I KEEP THROWING UP!

STACEY: I WAS GIVEN X-RAYS BY MY DENTIST YESTERDAY.

CASEY: OH, TOOTH PICS?

WHAT DO CATS EAT ON HOT DAYS?

MICE-CREAM CONES!

WHY ARE CATS SO GOOD AT EXAMS?

THEY GIVE PURRFECT ANSWERS!

HOW DO CATS KNOW WHAT IS GOING ON IN THE WORLD?

THEY READ THE MEWSPAPER!

WHY ARE THERE MORE GHOST CATS THAN GHOST DOGS?

BECAUSE EVERY CAT HAS NINE LIVES!

WHAT KIND OF PIZZA DO DOGS ORDER?

PUPPERONI!!

WHAT DO DOGS EAT FOR BREAKFAST?

POOCHED EGGS!

WHY DID THE DOG CHASE ITS OWN TAIL?

IT WAS TRYING TO MAKE BOTH ENDS MEET!

WHY DO DOGS BURY BONES IN THE GROUND?

BECAUSE YOU CAN'T BURY THEM IN TREES!

145

KNOCK, KNOCK...

WHO'S THERE?

SOMEONE ON A SWING.

TELL THEM TO GET OFF.

KNOCK, KNOCK...

WHO'S THERE?

SOMEONE SELLING HONEY.

TELL THEM TO BUZZ OFF.

KNOCK, KNOCK...

WHO'S THERE?

SOMEONE WITH A DRUM.

TELL THEM TO BEAT IT.

KNOCK, KNOCK...

WHO'S THERE?

A BOY SCOUT.

TELL THEM TO TAKE A HIKE.

WHAT DO YOU CALL A CAT THAT'S SWALLOWED A DUCK?

A DUCK-FILLED FATTY PUSS!

WHAT DO CATS PUT IN THEIR COLA?

UBES!

WHY ARE CATS SO GOOD AT PLAYING THE PIANO?

BECAUSE THEY ARE VERY MEW-SICAL!

WHO WON THE MILK-DRINKING COMPETITION?

THE CAT—IT LAPPED THE FIELD!

153

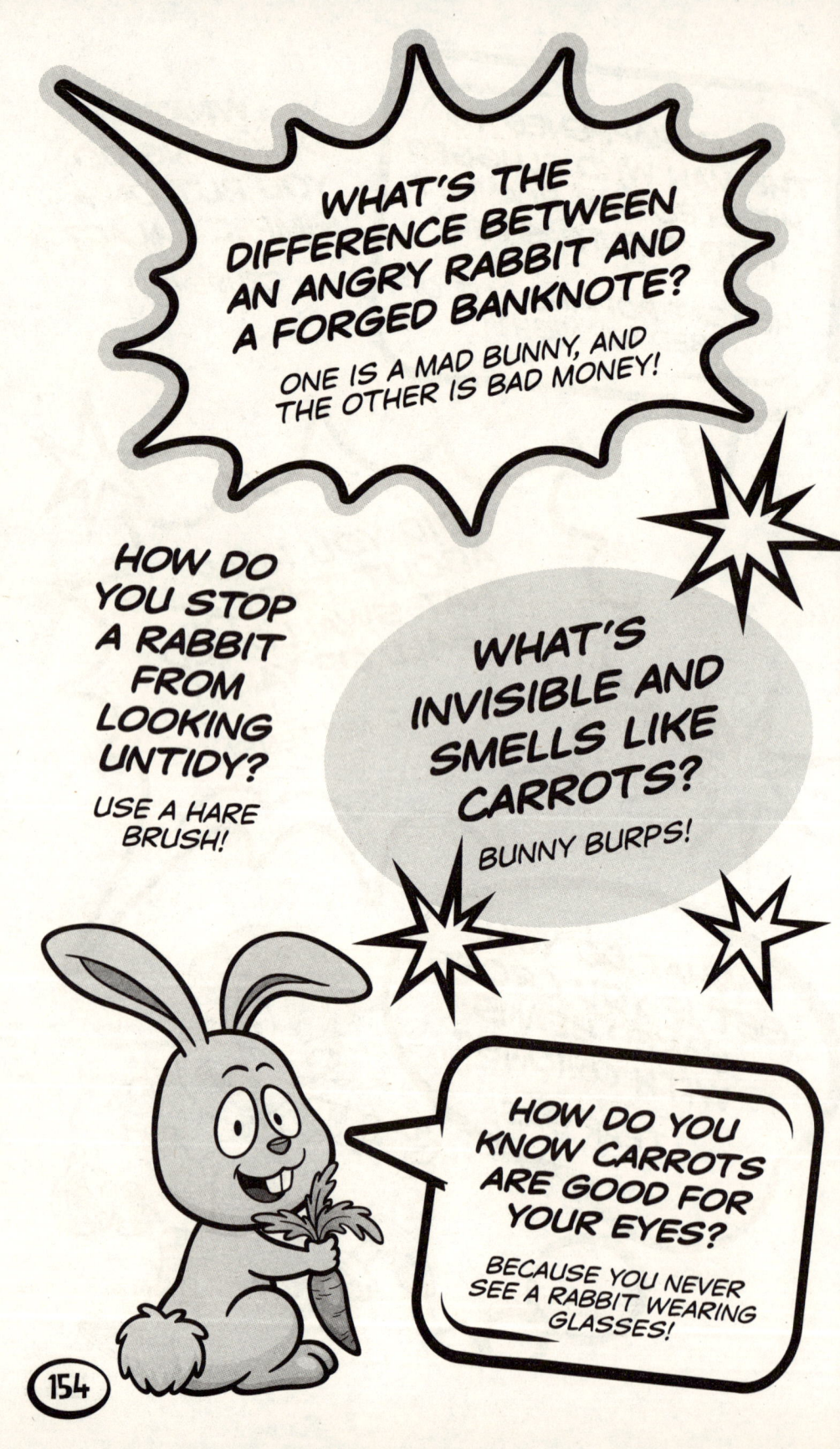

WHEN SHOULD A MOUSE STAY INDOORS?

WHEN IT'S RAINING CATS AND DOGS!

WHO ARE SMALL, FURRY, AND FANTASTIC AT SWORD FIGHTING?

THE THREE MOUSEKETEERS!

WHY SHOULDN'T YOU WORRY IF YOU SEE MICE IN YOUR HOME?

THEY'RE PROBABLY DOING THE MOUSEWORK!

WHAT DO YOU DO IF YOUR PET MOUSE FALLS IN THE SINK?

GIVE IT MOUSE-TO-MOUSE RESUSCITATION!

CASEY: WHY IS YOUR SISTER SO GOOD AT SPORT?

STACEY: SHE HAS ATHLETE'S FOOT!

WHY DID THE JOGGER EAT ON THE RUN?

SHE LOVED FAST FOOD!

AMANDA: IS YOUR BROTHER ANY GOOD AT RUNNING?

MIRANDA: HE'S SO SLOW HE RAN A BATH AND CAME SECOND!

WHEN IS A BASKETBALL PLAYER LIKE A BABY?

WHEN HE DRIBBLES!

RON: WHY ARE YOU TAKING PLANKS AND A HAMMER TO THE SPORTS HALL?

JOHN: I'M GOING FOR FENCING LESSONS!

DAD: WHAT SHADE IS YOUR NEW CHEERLEADING UNIFORM?

LUCY: YELLER!

FRANKIE: THERE ARE ONLY TWO THINGS STOPPING ME FROM GETTING ONTO THE SCHOOL SOCCER TEAM.

DAD: WHAT ARE THEY?

FRANKIE: MY FEET!

TED: MY BROTHER GOT REALLY KNOCKED AROUND IN HIS LAST BOXING MATCH.

NED: SORE LOSER?

THELMA: IF THAT PLANET IS MARS, WHAT'S THE ONE HIGHER UP?

VELMA: IS IT PA'S?

FRED: MY TEACHER SAYS I SHOULD TRAIN TO BE AN ASTRONAUT.

JED: NO, SHE SAID YOU'RE A REAL SPACE CADET...

WHICH RELATIVE VISITS ASTRONAUTS IN OUTER SPACE?

AUNTIE GRAVITY!

WHY ARE GRANDPA'S TEETH LIKE STARS?

BECAUSE THEY COME OUT AT NIGHT!

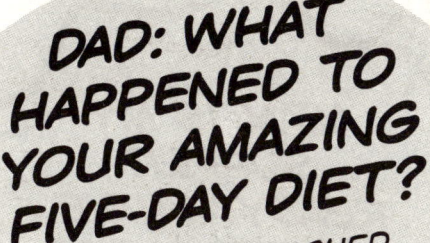

DAD: WHAT HAPPENED TO YOUR AMAZING FIVE-DAY DIET?

EDWARD: I FINISHED ALL THE FOOD IN TWO DAYS!

DREW: IF CAN'T IS SHORT FOR CANNOT, WHAT IS DON'T SHORT FOR?

SUE: DONUT?

WHAT'S THE DIFFERENCE BETWEEN A BORING PARENT AND A BORING BOOK?

YOU CAN SHUT THE BOOK UP!

DEAN: CAN WE WATCH THE CURSE OF THE BLACK PEARL TONIGHT?

JEAN: DAD WON'T LET US WATCH PIRATE DVDS.

ALAN: IS MY SUPPER READY? I HAVE KARATE CLASS IN AN HOUR.

MOTHER: YOUR CHOPS ARE ON THE TABLE!

EDWIN: I DON'T LIKE CHEESE WITH HOLES!

DAD: WELL, EAT THE CHEESE AND LEAVE THE HOLES ON THE SIDE OF YOUR PLATE.

WHY DID THE GIRL STARE AT THE CARTON OF ORANGE JUICE?

IT SAID "CONCENTRATE."

GRANDMA: EAT YOUR GREENS, THEY'RE GOOD FOR YOUR SKIN.

ALICE: BUT I DON'T WANT GREEN SKIN!

WHAT HAS A BOTTOM AT THE TOP?

THE TOILET!

WHY CAN'T YOU HEAR A PSYCHIATRIST GO TO THE BATHROOM?

BECAUSE THE P IS SILENT!

GRAN: WHY ARE YOU EATING THAT BAGUETTE IN THE BATHTUB?

STAN: IT'S A SUB SANDWICH!

WHAT DID THE BURGLAR'S DAUGHTER PLAY WITH AT BATHTIME?

A ROBBER DUCKY!

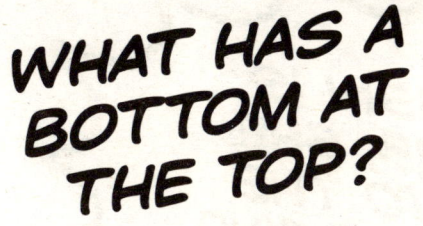

LITTLE PENCIL: YOU LOOK AS THOUGH YOU'VE PUT ON WEIGHT, DAD.

DADDY PENCIL: YOU'RE VERY BLUNT!

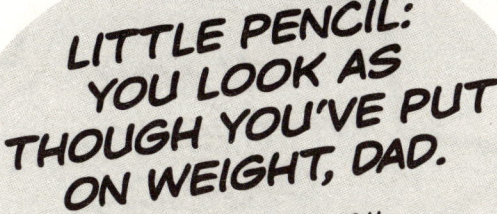

WHY WAS THE LITTLE BROOM LATE FOR SCHOOL?

IT OVERSWEPT!

WHY WAS THE LITTLE ICEBERG JUST LIKE HIS DAD?

BECAUSE HE WAS A CHIP OFF THE COLD BLOCK!

WHAT DID THE MOTHER DOG SAY TO THE PUPPY?

"WE'RE HAVING DINNER SOON, DON'T EAT TOO MUCH HOMEWORK!"

163

CLARK: WHY IS YOUR GRANDPA DRESSED AS A CLOWN?

MARK: JEST FOR FUN!

HOW DO YOU MAKE ANTIFREEZE?

HIDE HER COAT AND GLOVES!

MICKEY: OUR MOTHER HAS NAMED US ALL AFTER MEMBERS OF OUR FAMILY.

NICKY: IS THAT WHY YOUR BIG BROTHER IS CALLED UNCLE JOE?

DID YOU HEAR THAT UNCLE BOB LOST HIS WIG ON THE ROLLER COASTER?

IT WAS A HAIR-RAISING RIDE!

WHY DO LITTLE KIDS LISTEN TO THE RADIO ON LONG TRIPS?

BECAUSE CAR-TOONS KEEP THEM HAPPY!

JOSIE: MY SINGING TUTOR SAID MY VOICE IS HEAVENLY!

ROSIE: NOT REALLY – SHE SAID IT WAS LIKE NOTHING ON EARTH!

DID YOU HEAR ABOUT THE MAGICIAN WHO TRIED HIS SAWING-A-PERSON-IN-TWO TRICKS AT HOME?

HE HAD LOTS OF HALF BROTHERS AND SISTERS!

MOTHER: WHY DID YOU KICK YOUR BROTHER IN THE STOMACH?

SALLY: IT WAS AN ACCIDENT – HE TURNED AROUND!

165

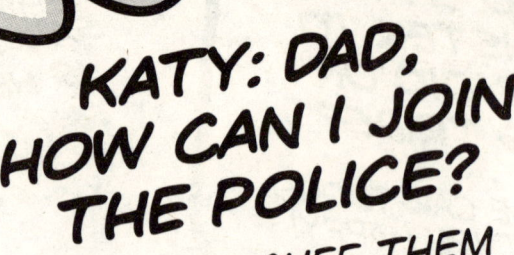

KATY: DAD, HOW CAN I JOIN THE POLICE?

DAD: HANDCUFF THEM ALL TOGETHER!

MATT: WHY DID YOUR DAD QUIT HIS JOB AT THE CAN CRUSHING PLANT?

KAT: BECAUSE IT WAS SODA PRESSING!

CHRIS: MY DAD'S AN UNDERTAKER.

FLISS: DOES HE ENJOY IT?

CHRIS: OF CORPSE HE DOES!

GRANDMA: WHAT DO YOU WANT TO BE WHEN YOU GROW UP, DEAR?

NATHANIEL: I'M ASPIRIN' TO BE A PHARMACIST!

CARRIE: DID YOU JUST FEED GARLIC BREAD TO OUR DOG?

HARRY: YES–ITS BARK IS MUCH WORSE THAN ITS BITE!

DANNY: MA, SHE'S STOLEN THE YOLK FROM MY EGG!

ANNIE: SHH, IT'S ALL WHITE NOW!

DAD: WHY DO YOUR SHOES LOOK LIKE BANANAS?

HARRIET: THEY'RE MY SLIPPERS!

MOTHER: WHAT DO IDK, LY AND TTYL MEAN?

DAUGHTER: I DON'T KNOW, LOVE YOU, TALK TO YOU LATER.

MOTHER: WELL, I'LL HAVE TO ASK YOUR SISTER THEN!

WHAT DO YOU GET IF YOU CROSS A DOG AND A FROG?

A PET THAT CAN LICK YOU FROM THE OTHER SIDE OF THE ROAD!

WHAT INSTRUMENT DO DOGS LIKE BEST?

THE TROM-BONE!

WHAT DO YOU GET IF YOU CROSS A COCKER SPANIEL, A POODLE, AND A ROOSTER?

COCKERPOODLEDOO!

WHAT HAPPENED TO THE DOG THAT SWALLOWED A FIREFLY?

IT BARKED WITH DE-LIGHT!

WHAT DO YOU GIVE YOUR PET RAT TO EAT?

RATATOUILLE!

WHY DO RATS HAVE LONG TAILS? BECAUSE THEY'D LOOK SILLY WITH LONG HAIR!

WHAT DO YOU GIVE TO A BABY RAT?

A RATTLE!

WHAT DO YOU CALL AN ANNOYING PET RAT?

A BRAT!

DAD: WHY DID YOU OVERSLEEP THIS MORNING?

TOBY: I WAS DREAMING ABOUT PLAYING FOOTBALL, AND IT WENT INTO EXTRA TIME!

NED: WHY IS THE LIGHT ALWAYS ON IN YOUR BROTHER'S ROOM?

FRED: BECAUSE HE'S SO DIM!

DAD: HAVE YOU HAD YOUR HOMEWORK MARKED YET?

BECKY: YES, I'M AFRAID YOU DIDN'T DO VERY WELL!

FLO: WHY ARE YOU CRYING AND CHEWING AT THE SAME TIME?

JOE: I JUST SWALLOWED SOME BLUBBER GUM!

CHLOE: HOW COME YOU'RE SO GOOD AT TENNIS?

ZOE: IT'S NOT RACKET SCIENCE!

MARK: WHY HAVE YOU VOLUNTEERED FOR HIGH JUMP FOR THE FIRST TIME EVER?

CLARK: I THOUGHT I MIGHT DO WELL AS IT'S A LEAP YEAR!

FLORENCE: WHY DO YOU ONLY PLAY BASEBALL AT NIGHT?

I HAVE A VAMPIRE BAT!

BOBBY: WHAT POSITION DOES YOUR BROTHER PLAY ON THE TEAM?

ROBBIE: I THINK HE'S ONE OF THE DRAWBACKS!

HOW DID VIKINGS SEND SECRET MESSAGES?

THEY USED NORSE CODE!

WHY DID THE VIKING NEED CHEERING UP?

HE HAD A SINKING FEELING.

WHERE DID THE TEACHER SEND THE VIKING WHEN HE GOT SICK IN CLASS?

TO THE SCHOOL NORSE!

WHEN DID THE VIKINGS MAKE THEIR RAIDS?

DURING A PLUNDER STORM!

WHICH CAT DISCOVERED AMERICA?

CHRISTOFUR COLUMPUSS!

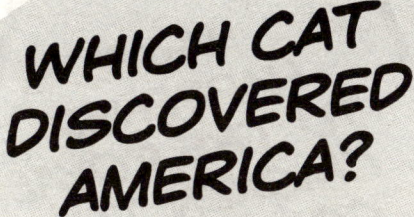

WHAT BUS SAILED ACROSS THE ATLANTIC?

CHRISTOPHER COLUM-BUS!

HOW DID CHRISTOPHER COLUMBUS GET TO COLLEGE?

ON A SCHOLAR-SHIP!

WHAT WERE THE FIRST ISLANDS COLUMBUS SIGHTED?

THE AHA!-MAS!

WHAT HAPPENED TO THE ROYAL CHICKEN THAT COULDN'T LAY EGGS?
THE KING HAD HER EGGS-ECUTED!

WHY DID THE KING VISIT THE DENTIST?
TO HAVE HIS TEETH CROWNED!

WHAT DID KING HENRY VIII DO WHENEVER HE BURPED?
HE ISSUED A ROYAL PARDON!

WHY DID EVERYONE IN 19TH-CENTURY ENGLAND CARRY AN UMBRELLA?
BECAUSE QUEEN VICTORIA'S REIGN LASTED FOR 64 YEARS!

WHAT WAS THE FIRST THING QUEEN VICTORIA DID ON ASCENDING TO THE THRONE?

SAT DOWN!

WHAT DO YOU CALL IT WHEN THE QUEEN GOES TO THE BATHROOM?

A ROYAL FLUSH!

WHAT DID ANNE BOLEYN'S LADY IN WAITING SAY ON HER WEDDING DAY?

"THAT MAN'S NOT WORTH LOSING YOUR HEAD OVER!"

WHY DID THEY CALL KING ALFRED "THE GREAT?"

BECAUSE ALFRED THE FANTASTIC SOUNDED WRONG!

WHY COULDN'T THE ANIMALS PLAY CARDS ON NOAH'S ARK?

BECAUSE NOAH WAS STANDING ON THE DECK!

HOW DID NOAH NAVIGATE IN THE DARK?

HE USED FLOODLIGHTS!

WHAT DID NOAH DO FOR A LIVING?

HE WAS AN ARK-ITECT!

WHAT HAPPENED WHEN THEY FINALLY GOT THE CARDS ON NOAH'S ARK?

THEIR GAME WAS RUINED BY TWO CHEETAHS!

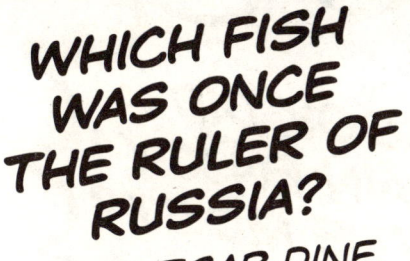

WHICH FISH WAS ONCE THE RULER OF RUSSIA?

THE TSAR-DINE.

WHICH RUSSIAN LEADER WAS A BIG FAN OF FRUIT?

PETER THE GRAPE!

TEACHER: CAN YOU TELL ME WHAT NATIONALITY NAPOLEON WAS?

FIONA: COURSE I CAN!

WHICH EMPEROR SHOULD HAVE STAYED AWAY FROM GUNPOWDER?

NAPOLEON BLOWNAPART!

WHICH BOOK DID MARK TWAIN ENJOY WRITING THE MOST?

HUCKLEBERRY FUN!

HOW DID THE HUNCHBACK OF NOTRE DAME CURE HIS SORE THROAT?

HE GARGOYLED!

HOW DID NEIL ARMSTRONG SAY HE WAS SORRY?

HE APOLLO-GIZED!

WHAT DO YOU CALL A FORTUNATE DETECTIVE?

SHEERLUCK HOLMES!

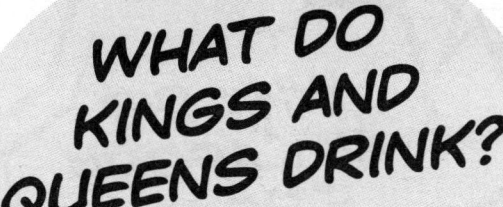

WHAT DO KINGS AND QUEENS DRINK?

ROYAL-TEA!

WHICH GORILLA HAD SIX WIVES?

HENRY THE APE!

WHAT WAS QUEEN VICTORIA'S MOST TREASURED ITEM OF CLOTHING?

HER REIGN-COAT!

WHAT DID QUEEN VICTORIA SAY WHEN SHE STEPPED IN COW DUNG?

"WE ARE NOT A-MOO-SED!"

WHO RIDES A HORSE, WEARS A MASK, AND SMELLS GOOD?

THE COLOGNE RANGER!

WHAT DO YOU CALL A FROG WHO WANTS TO BE A COWBOY?

HOPPALONG CASSIDY!

MR. MONEY: I ASKED MY CLASS TO NAME A CREATURE THAT WAS HALF-MAN AND HALF-BEAST.

MR. HONEY: SO DID I. THEY SAID BUFFALO BILL.

WHY DID THE COWBOY CHOOSE HIS HORSE IN DAYTIME?

HE DIDN'T WANT NIGHTMARES!

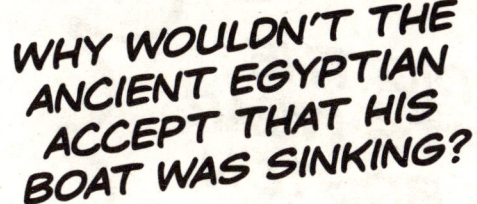

WHY WOULDN'T THE ANCIENT EGYPTIAN ACCEPT THAT HIS BOAT WAS SINKING?

HE WAS IN DE!

WHY WERE THE ANCIENT EGYPTIANS GOOD AT SPYING?

THEY KEPT THINGS UNDER WRAPS!

WHY DIDN'T THE ANCIENT EGYPTIANS HAVE DOORBELLS?

THEY JUST TOOT-AND-COME-IN!

HOW DO YOU FIND TUTANKHAMEN'S TOMB?

PEER-AMID THE OTHER TOMBS!

WHAT DID THE COLONISTS WEAR AT THE BOSTON TEA PARTY?

TEA-SHIRTS!

WHY DIDN'T GEORGE WASHINGTON BOTHER GOING TO BED?

BECAUSE HE COULDN'T LIE!

WHAT KIND OF TEA WERE THE COLONISTS LOOKING FOR?

LIBER-TEA!

WHERE DID THE PILGRIMS LAND WHEN THEY ARRIVED IN AMERICA?

ON THE BEACH!

WHAT DO YOU GET IF YOU CROSS A ROMAN EMPEROR WITH A BOA CONSTRICTOR?

JULIUS SQUEEZER!

WHO WOULD REFEREE A TENNIS MATCH BETWEEN JULIUS CAESAR AND BRUTUS?

A ROMAN UMPIRE!

WHICH ROMAN EMPEROR WAS THE COOLEST?

JULIUS FREEZER!

WHICH ROMAN EMPEROR WAS ASTHMATIC?

JULIUS WHEEZER!

TEACHER: CAN YOU THINK OF AN ANCIENT MUSICAL INSTRUMENT?

JAKE: AN ANGLO-SAXOPHONE?

WHICH MONARCH HAD THE WORST SKIN?

MARY QUEEN OF SPOTS!

DID YOU HEAR ABOUT THE QUEEN WHOSE ELDEST SON DISOBEYED HER?

SHE WAS HAVING A BAD HEIR DAY!

DAWN: I WISH I'D BEEN BORN 500 YEARS AGO.

SHAUN: WHY'S THAT?

DAWN: SO I WOULDN'T HAVE TO LEARN SO MUCH HISTORY!

WHAT DOES AN EXECUTIONER READ IN THE MORNING?

THE NOOSE-PAPER!

WHAT DID THE EXECUTIONER SAY TO THE PRISONER?

"TIME TO HEAD OFF!"

WHAT DID THE EXECUTIONER SHOUT TO THE LINE OF PRISONERS?

"NECKS, PLEASE!"

WHAT DO YOU GET IF YOU CROSS A HANGMAN AND A CIRCUS PERFORMER?

SOMEONE WHO GOES STRAIGHT FOR THE JUGGLER!

WHY DID THE ARCHER CHANGE HIS CAREER?

HE FOUND HIS JOB TOO ARROWING!

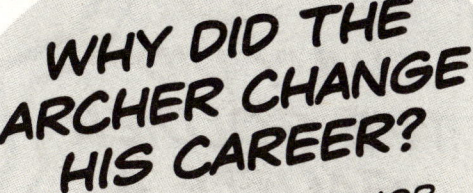

WHAT WOULD YOU GET HANGING FROM CASTLE WALLS?

TIRED ARMS!

WHY DID THE HANGMAN'S WIFE ASK FOR A DIVORCE?

HER HUSBAND WAS A PAIN IN THE NECK!

WHY DID SOLDIERS FIRE ARROWS FROM THE CASTLE?

THEY WERE TRYING TO GET THEIR POINT ACROSS!

WHY DID THE SOLDIER SALUTE A TIGER?

IT HAD MORE STRIPES!

WHY DID THE SOLDIER PUT A TANK IN HIS HOUSE?

IT WAS A FISH TANK!

DID YOU HEAR ABOUT THE KARATE CHAMPION WHO JOINED THE ARMY?

THE FIRST TIME HE SALUTED, HE KNOCKED HIMSELF OUT!

MAJOR: I DIDN'T SEE YOU IN CAMOUFLAGE TRAINING THIS MORNING, PRIVATE!

PRIVATE: THANK YOU VERY MUCH, SIR!

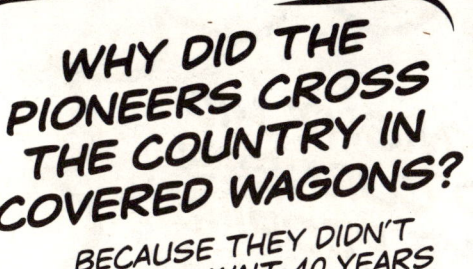

WHY DID THE PIONEERS CROSS THE COUNTRY IN COVERED WAGONS?

BECAUSE THEY DIDN'T WANT TO WAIT 40 YEARS FOR A TRAIN!

WHERE DO COWBOYS COOK THEIR MEALS?

ON THE RANGE.

WHY DID THE COWBOY RIDE A HORSE?

IT WAS TOO HEAVY TO CARRY!

WHAT DID THE COWBOY SAY WHEN HIS DOG LEFT?

"DOGGONE!"

WHY DID THE ROMANS BUILD SUCH STRAIGHT ROADS?

SO THEIR SOLDIERS DIDN'T GO AROUND THE BEND!

NERO: WHAT TIME IS IT?

SERVANT: X PAST V!

WHAT DO YOU SAY TO GET ROMANS TO SING ALONG?

"ALL TOGA-ETHER NOW!"

WHAT DO YOU CALL A ROMAN EMPEROR WHO HAS ADVENTURES?

AN ACTION NERO!

207

WHICH ENGLISHMAN INVENTED FRACTIONS?

HENRY THE EIGHTH!

WHO INVENTED MATCHES?

SOME BRIGHT SPARK!

WHAT HAPPENED WHEN THE WHEEL WAS INVENTED?

IT CAUSED A REVOLUTION!

WHAT HAPPENED WHEN ELECTRICITY WAS FIRST DISCOVERED?

PEOPLE GOT A NASTY SHOCK!

WHICH ANIMAL INVENTED THE INTERNET?

THE BEAVER, SINCE IT WAS THE FIRST TO LOG ON!

WHAT INVENTION LETS YOU SEE THROUGH WALLS?

THE WINDOW!

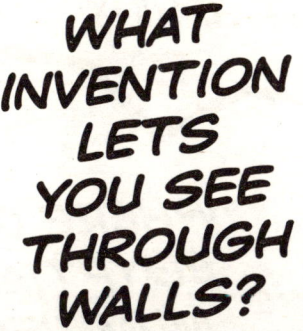

WHAT WAS THE NAME OF THE INVENTOR OF THE COMPUTER?

CHIP!

WHAT WAS THE FIRST THING SAID BY THE INVENTOR OF THE STINK BOMB?

"YOU REEK, UGH!"

DID YOU HEAR ABOUT THE UNEMBALMED ANCIENT EGYPTIAN DISCOVERY?

IT SPHINX!

WHAT WAS THE SCORE AT THE ANCIENT EGYPTIAN SOCCER GAME?

ONE-NILE!

WHERE DO EGYPTIAN MUMMIES GO FOR A SWIM?

THE DEAD SEA!

IN WHICH PART OF A TOMB DID THE ANCIENT EGYPTIANS BURY THE DEAD?

IN THE PYRA-MIDDLE!

WHY WAS THE PHARAOH SO TENSE?

HE WAS GETTING WOUND UP!

WHY DID THE MUMMY CALL THE DOCTOR?

BECAUSE HE WAS COFFIN!

WHAT KIND OF JEWELS DID THE ANCIENT EGYPTIANS DECORATE THEIR COFFINS WITH?

TOMB-STONES!

DID YOU HEAR ABOUT THE MUMMY THAT LOST ITS TEMPER?

IT FLIPPED ITS LID!

211

WHICH ANCIENT GREEK WAS THE BEST OF THE BUNCH?

ALEXANDER THE GRAPE!

WHY WAS THE BULLHEADED CREATURE NOT ALLOWED TO VOTE?

BECAUSE IT WAS ONLY A MINOR-TAUR!

WHICH FRUIT LAUNCHED A THOUSAND SHIPS?

MELON OF TROY!

WHAT MOVIE DID THE ANCIENT GREEKS LIKE BEST?

TROY STORY!

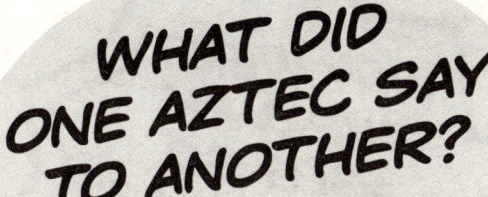

WHAT DID ONE AZTEC SAY TO ANOTHER?

WE ALL HAVE TO MAKE SACRIFICES!

WHY DID SIR WALTER RALEIGH SAIL TO SOUTH AMERICA?

IT WAS TOO FAR TO SWIM!

WHERE DID MONTEZUMA GO TO COLLEGE?

AZ TECH!

WHEN DID MONTEZUMA DIE?

A FEW DAYS BEFORE THEY BURIED HIM!

WHY WERE THE DARK AGES SO CONFUSING?

IT WAS COMMON TO HEAR, "GOOD MORNING, GOOD KNIGHT!"

SHIRLEY: WHEN WAS THE MAGNA CARTA SIGNED?

HURLEY: 1215.

SHIRLEY: OH, JUST BEFORE LUNCH THEN!

WHY WERE BRITISH PEOPLE REALLY TANNED OVER 2,000 YEARS AGO?

THEY LIVED IN THE BRONZED AGE!

WHAT WAS IN FASHION AT THE TIME OF THE GREAT FIRE OF LONDON?

BLAZERS!

SILLY CELEBRATIONS

WHY DID THE SCIENTIST USE A MICROSCOPE TO READ HIS VALENTINE CARD?

BECAUSE IT WAS VALEN-TINY!

WHY DO SKUNKS LOVE VALENTINE'S DAY?

BECAUSE THEY'RE SCENT-IMENTAL!

WHAT DID THE RECTANGLE WRITE IN THE TRIANGLE'S VALENTINE?

"I THINK YOU'RE ACUTE!"

HOW DID THE SKELETON KNOW HE HAD FOUND TRUE LOVE?

HE FELT IT IN HIS BONES!

HOW MUCH DOES A SLOBBERY DOG LOVE ITS OWNER?
DROOLY, MADLY, DEEPLY!

WHAT DID THE LIGHTBULB SAY TO THE SWITCH?
"YOU LIGHT UP MY LIFE!"

WHAT KIND OF FOOD IS SUITED TO VALENTINE'S DAY?
A HEARTY MEAL!

WHY DID THE TORTOISES GET MARRIED?
BECAUSE THEY WERE TURTLE-Y IN LOVE!

WHAT SORT OF JOKES DO EASTER CHICKS LIKE?

CORNY ONES!

WHERE DO YOU FIND THE BEST EASTER EGG JOKES?

IN A YOLK BOOK!

WHAT KIND OF PEOPLE ARE THE BEST AT EASTER EGG HUNTS?

EGGSPLORERS!

WHAT DID THE EASTER BUNNY SAY TO THE CARROT?

"IT'S BEEN NICE GNAWING YOU!"

HOW DOES THE EASTER BUNNY STAY FIT?

EGGS-ERCISE!

WHAT'S THE BEST WAY TO CATCH THE EASTER BUNNY?

HIDE IN A BUSH AND MAKE A NOISE LIKE A CARROT!

HOW CAN YOU SEND A LETTER TO THE EASTER BUNNY?

BY HARE MAIL!

WHAT DO YOU CALL A LINE OF RABBITS WHO'VE BEEN WAITING IN THE SUN FOR TOO LONG?

HOT CROSS BUNNIES!

WHY CAN'T YOU TAKE A TURKEY TO CHURCH?

BECAUSE THEY USE SUCH FOWL LANGUAGE!

WHEN DOES CHRISTMAS COME BEFORE THANKSGIVING?

IN THE DICTIONARY!

WHAT SMELLS THE BEST AT A THANKSGIVING DINNER?

YOUR NOSE!

WHAT SHOULD YOU WEAR TO THANKSGIVING DINNER?

A HAR-VEST!

WHAT DO MATHEMATICIANS EAT FOR THANKSGIVING DINNER?

PUMPKIN PI!

WHY ARE TURKEYS WISER THAN CHICKENS?

EVER HEARD OF KENTUCKY FRIED TURKEY?!

WHY DID THE TURKEY WANT TO JOIN A BAND?

BECAUSE HE ALREADY HAD THE DRUMSTICKS!

WHAT DID THE TURKEY SAY WHEN IT SAW THE FARMER?

"QUACK, QUACK!"

WHERE IS THE BEST PLACE TO GO ON HALLOWEEN?

THE SCREAM PARK!

WHICH RIDE DO GHOSTS ENJOY THE MOST?

THE ROLLER GHOSTER!

WHERE IN A HAUNTED HOUSE WILL YOU AVOID ALL THE GHOSTS?

THE LIVING ROOM!

WHY DIDN'T THE GHOST TRY TO WIN A CUDDLY TOY?

HE DIDN'T HAVE A GHOST OF A CHANCE!

WHY COULDN'T THE ELF WORK IN SANTA'S TOYSHOP?

HE HAD TINSELITUS!

HOW DO ELVES GET TO THE TOP FLOOR?

AN ELF-AVATOR!

IF SANTA TRAVELS IN A SLEIGH, WHAT DO HIS ELVES TRAVEL IN?

A MINIVAN!

WHERE DO THE ELVES GO TO DANCE?

A SNOWBALL!

225

WHO DRESSES
IN RED AND WHITE,
AND IS A DANGER IN
THE WATER?

SANTA JAWS!

HOW
MUCH DID
SANTA PAY
FOR HIS
SLEIGH?

NOTHING, IT
WAS ON THE
HOUSE!

WHAT DO
SNOWMEN
SING TO
SANTA CLAUS?

"FREEZE A JOLLY
GOOD FELLOW!"

WHAT DO YOU
SHOUT WHEN
SANTA TAKES
THE ROLL CALL?

"PRESENT!"

WHAT DO REINDEER HANG ON THEIR CHRISTMAS TREES?

HORN-AMENTS!

WHAT DO GHOSTS PUT ON THEIR TURKEY AT CHRISTMAS?

GRAVE-Y!

WHAT SNEAKS AROUND THE KITCHEN ON CHRISTMAS EVE?

MINCE SPIES!

WHAT CAN YOU SEE FLYING THROUGH THE SKY ON CHRISTMAS EVE?

A U.F. HO-HO-HO!

WHAT DID THE BOA CONSTRICTOR WRITE IN ITS VALENTINE CARD?

"I HAVE A CRUSH ON YOU!"

WHAT SONG DOES A BULL SING ON VALENTINE'S DAY?

"WHEN I FALL IN LOVE...IT WILL BE FOR HEIFER."

WHAT DID ONE STAR SAY TO ANOTHER STAR?

"DO YOU WANT TO GLOW ON A DATE?"

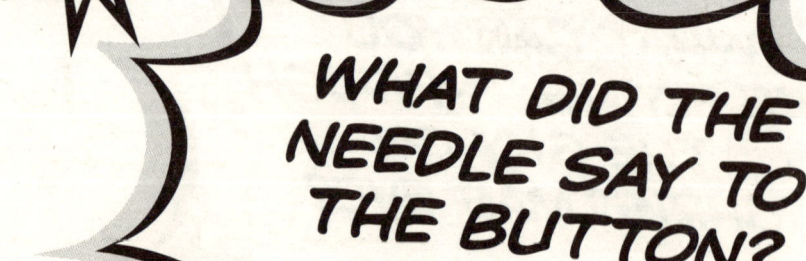

WHAT DID THE NEEDLE SAY TO THE BUTTON?

"I LOVE YOU SEW MUCH!"

DID YOU HEAR THAT THE EASTER BUNNY WON THE LOTTERY?

HE'S A MILLION-HARE!

WHAT TAKEOUT DOES THE EASTER BUNNY USUALLY ORDER?

HOP SUEY!

WHAT DO YOU CALL THE EASTER BUNNY IF HE HAS FLEAS?

BUGS BUNNY!

WHAT KIND OF MUSIC DOES THE EASTER BUNNY LISTEN TO?

HIP-HOP!

WHY WAS THE CHICKEN STRESSED?

BECAUSE SHE'D MISLAID HER EGGS!

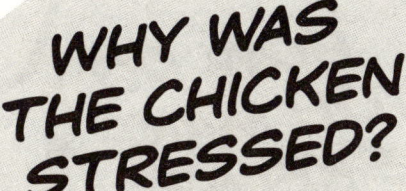

WHY DID THE CHICKEN VISIT THE DOCTOR?

IT WAS FEELING FOWL!

IN WHICH DIRECTION DO YOU HEAD TO FIND CHOCOLATE EGGS?

A LITTLE EASTER HERE!

WHY DID THE EASTER BUNNY WANT TO MOVE?

HE WAS FED UP OF THE HOLE THING!

WHAT GAME DO VAMPIRES LOVE TO PLAY?

CASKETBALL!

WHY ARE GRAVEYARDS SUCH NOISY PLACES?

BECAUSE OF ALL THE COFFIN!

WHAT DID THE GHOST SAY TO HER SON AS THEY DROVE AWAY FROM HOME?

FASTEN YOUR SHEET BELT!

WHAT DO YOU CALL A VAMPIRE THAT EATS ALL THE TIME?

SNACKULA!

WHAT DID THE WOODCUTTER'S WIFE SAY TO HER HUSBAND ON DECEMBER 1ST?

"NOT MANY CHOPPING DAYS LEFT UNTIL CHRISTMAS!"

HOW DID JACK FROST BREAK HIS WRIST?

HE FELL OFF HIS ICICLE!

HAVE YOU HEARD THE SILLY STORY ABOUT A GIANT MINCE PIE?

IT'S VERY HARD TO SWALLOW.

WHO DELIVERS PRESENTS TO PETS?

SANTA CLAWS!

WHAT DO ANGRY MICE SEND EACH OTHER AT CHRISTMAS?

CROSS-MOUSE CARDS!

WHAT DO YOU GET IF YOU CROSS AN APPLE WITH A CHRISTMAS TREE?

A PINEAPPLE!

DOCTOR, I CAN'T SLEEP BECAUSE I AM SO EXCITED ABOUT CHRISTMAS!

LIE ON THE EDGE OF YOUR BED, AND YOU'LL SOON DROP OFF!

WHAT DOES MOWGLI SING AT CHRISTMAS?

"JUNGLE BELLS, JUNGLE BELLS..."

WHAT DID ONE SNOWMAN SAY TO THE OTHER?

"CAN YOU SMELL CARROTS?"

WHAT DO YOU GET IN DECEMBER THAT YOU DON'T GET IN ANY OTHER MONTH?

THE LETTER D!

HOW DOES GOOD KING WENCESLAS LIKE HIS PIZZA?

DEEP PAN, CRISP, AND EVEN!

WHAT'S WHITE AND GOES UP?

A STUPID SNOWFLAKE!

WHAT IS IMPOSSIBLE TO PASS AT CHRISTMAS?

THE THREE WIDE MEN!

HOW DOES CHRISTMAS DAY END?

WITH THE LETTER "Y"!

WHAT DO YOU GET IF SANTA COMES DOWN THE CHIMNEY WHEN THE FIRE IS LIT?

CRISP CRINGLE!

HOW DO YOU START A SANTA RACE?

ON YOUR MARKS, GET SET, HO HO HO!

WHAT WAS THE CHEF'S SECRET INGREDIENT FOR LOVE?

VALEN-THYME!

DID YOU HEAR ABOUT THE COUPLE WHO MET IN A REVOLVING DOOR?

THEY'RE STILL GOING AROUND TOGETHER!

WHAT MESSAGE WAS INSIDE THE RABBIT'S VALENTINE CARD?

SOME BUNNY LOVES YOU!

WHAT DID THE PIG FARMER GIVE HIS WIFE ON VALENTINE'S DAY?

HOGS AND KISSES!

238

WHAT DID THE SNAIL WRITE IN THE VALENTINE'S CARD?

"BE MY VALEN-SLIME!"

WHAT KIND OF FLOWERS ARE NO GOOD FOR VALENTINE'S DAY?

CAULIFLOWERS!

HARRY: DO YOU HAVE A DATE FOR THE VALENTINE BALL?

CARRIE: YES, FEBRUARY 14TH!

WHAT DID THE FRENCH CHEF GIVE HIS GIRLFRIEND ON VALENTINE'S DAY?

A HUG AND A QUICHE!

WHAT KIND OF EASTER EGGS DO ALIENS HAVE?

EGGS-TRATERRESTRIAL ONES!

WHO VISITS MERMAIDS AT EASTER?

THE OYSTER BUNNY!

WHAT DO YOU CALL IT WHEN CHICKS EAT OUTDOORS?

A PECK-NIC!

WHAT TIME DO CHICKENS WAKE UP?

SIX O'CLUCK!

WHY DON'T SKELETONS LIKE THANKSGIVING?

THEY HAVEN'T ANY BODY TO SPEND IT WITH!

WHAT DO VAMPIRES SING ON NEW YEAR'S EVE?

AULD FANG SYNE!

WHY DIDN'T THE SKELETON TELL HIS VALENTINE HE LOVED HER?

HE DIDN'T HAVE THE GUTS!

WHEN DO GHOSTS PLAY TRICKS ON EACH OTHER?

APRIL GHOUL'S DAY!

WHAT MONSTER PLAYS TRICKS ON HALLOWEEN?

PRANK-ENSTEIN!

WHAT DO GHOULS PUT ON THEIR BAGELS?

SCREAM CHEESE!

WHAT DID THE UNHAPPY GHOST SAY?

"BOO-HOO!"

WHAT DO YOU CALL A NATIVE AMERICAN GHOST?

POCA-HAUNT-US!

WHY DID THE GHOST GO UP THE STAIRS?

TO RAISE ITS SPIRITS!

WHAT DOES A SHORT-SIGHTED GHOST NEED?

SPOOK-TACLES!

WHAT CAN YOU HEAR AT HALLOWEEN SAYING, "BITE, SLURP, OUCH!"?

A VAMPIRE WITH A TOOTHACHE!

WHY COULDN'T THE GHOST FIND ITS DAD?

BECAUSE HE WAS TRANSPARENT!

245

HOW MANY LEGS DOES A REINDEER HAVE?

SIX – FORELEGS AT THE FRONT AND TWO AT THE BACK!

WHAT GOES "OH, OH, OH?"

SANTA WALKING BACKWARD!

WHAT'S RED AND WHITE, AND RED AND WHITE, AND RED AND WHITE?

SANTA STUCK IN A REVOLVING DOOR!

WHAT DID THE SHEEP SAY TO THE SHEPHERDS AT CHRISTMAS?

SEASONS BLEATINGS!

WHY DID SANTA GET A PARKING TICKET?

HE LEFT HIS SLEIGH IN A SNOW PARKING ZONE!

WHAT DOES MRS. CLAUS SAY WHEN SHE SEES BLACK CLOUDS?

"LOOKS LIKE RAIN, DEAR!"

WHAT DOES JACK FROST LIKE BEST AT SCHOOL?

SNOW AND TELL!

WHAT DOES SANTA WRITE ON FUNNY TEXT MESSAGES?

HHHOL!

WHERE DO YOU FIND THE MOST FAMOUS MISTLETOE?

HOLLY-WOOD!

WHAT CAROL DO SKUNKS SING?

JINGLE SMELLS!

HOW DOES SANTA KNOW WHAT PRESENTS TO GIVE EACH PERSON?

HE LOOKS FOR THE SANTA CLUES!

WHAT IS THE GRAMMATICALLY CORRECT TERM FOR SANTA'S ELVES?

SUBORDINATE CLAUSES!

WHAT DID THE SKELETON WRITE IN HER VALENTINE CARD?

"I LOVE EVERY BONE IN YOUR BODY!"

WHAT DID THE MAGNET SAY TO HER BOYFRIEND?

"YOU'RE VERY ATTRACTIVE!"

WHAT DID THE STAG SAY TO HIS GIRLFRIEND?

"I LOVE YOU DEERLY!"

WHAT DID THE GYMNAST SAY TO HER VALENTINE?

"I'M HEAD OVER HEELS IN LOVE WITH YOU!"

250

WHAT DO VAMPIRES DO AT THE END OF THE SCHOOL YEAR?

BLOOD TESTS!

WHAT DRINK DID THE GHOST ORDER AT THE DRIVE-THROUGH?

BOO-NANA MILK SHAKE!

WHAT DID THE GHOST SAY TO HIS GIRLFRIEND?

"YOU LOOK BOO-TIFUL TONIGHT!"

WHEN DOES A GHOST EAT BREAKFAST?

IN THE MOANING!

WHY IS IT SO COLD AT CHRISTMAS?

BECAUSE IT'S DECEMBRRRR!

WHAT DO YOU CALL SOMEONE WHO STEALS GIFT WRAP FROM THE RICH AND GIVES IT TO THE POOR?

RIBBON HOOD!

WHAT DID MRS. CLAUS SAY WHEN SANTA SHED A TEAR?

"DON'T GET SO SANTA-MENTAL, DARLING!"

WHAT KIND OF BALL DOESN'T BOUNCE?

A SNOWBALL!

WHY WAS SANTA'S LITTLE HELPER SO SAD?

BECAUSE HE HAD LOW ELF ESTEEM!

WHAT DID THE CANDLE SAY TO THE OTHER CANDLE?

"I'M GOING OUT TONIGHT!"

WHAT DID THE CHRISTMAS TREE SAY TO THE DECORATIONS?

"AREN'T YOU TIRED OF JUST HANGING AROUND?"

WHAT DO SNOWMEN LIKE TO DO AFTER CHRISTMAS?

CHILL OUT!